Cars, Curfews, Parties, and Parents...

77 Pretty Important Ideas

Lockers, Lunchlines, Chemistry and Cliques
Cars, Curfews, Parties and Parents

Cars, Curfews, Parties, and Parents...

SUSIE SHELLENBERGER
& GREG JOHNSON

BETHANY HOUSE PUBLISHERS
MINNEAPOLIS, MINNESOTA 55438

Published by Bethany House Publishers
A Ministry of Bethany Fellowship, Inc.
11300 Hampshire Avenue South
Minneapolis, Minnesota 55438

Printed in the United States of America.

Library of Congress Cataloging-in-Publication Data

Shellenberger, Susie.
Cars, curfews, parties, and parents : 77 pretty important ideas for family survival / Susie Shellenberger, Greg Johnson.
p. cm. — (77 pretty important ideas for survival)
Summary: Explores all-important family issues of importance to teens such as obedience to parents, dating, choosing friends, etc.

1. Parent and teenager—Juvenile literature. 2. Parent and teenager—Religious aspects—Christianity—Juvenile literature. 3. Teenagers—Family relationships—Juvenile literature. 4. Teenagers—Religious life—Juvenile literature. 5. Adolescence—Juvenile literature. [1. Parent and child. 2. Family life. 3. Christian life. I. Johnson, Greg. II. Title. III. Series: Shellenberger, Susie. 77 pretty important ideas for survival.
HQ799.15.S54 1994
649'.125—dc20 94–49217
ISBN 1–55661–482–9 CIP
AC

Dedicated to . . .

Woodie and Cheryl Stevens

and

Stanley and Susan Woodard

Thank you for including *me* in your families.

My life is richer because of your love.

—Susie Shellenberger

SUSIE SHELLENBERGER is the editor of *Brio* magazine for teen girls (cir. 160,000), published by FOCUS ON THE FAMILY. A graduate of SOUTHERN NAZARENE UNIVERSITY and the UNIVERSITY OF CENTRAL OKLAHOMA, Susie's experience with teens ranges from youth ministry to teaching high school speech and drama. She is the author of nine books, including *There's a Sheep in My Mirror* and *Straight Ahead.*

GREG JOHNSON is the former editor of *Breakaway* magazine for teen boys (cir. 90,000) and the author or co-author of fifteen books, including *If I Could Ask God One Question* and *Daddy's Home.* A graduate of NORTHWEST CHRISTIAN COLLEGE, Greg has been involved with teens for over fifteen years and has worked with YOUTH FOR CHRIST and FOCUS ON THE FAMILY. He and his wife have two sons and make their home in Colorado Springs, where Greg is a literary agent for ALIVE COMMUNICATIONS.

Adjusting to your HORMONES takes time.

Maybe you know it. Maybe you don't. But there's a silent alarm clock ticking inside your body. Its name—**puberty.**

This alarm goes off at different times for every teen. Sometime between the ages of eleven and fourteen, obvious physical changes take place. These physical changes are usually accompanied by a roller coaster of emotions . . . emotions that can set a parent and teen at each other's throats!

It doesn't take much to trigger a powerful emotional reaction. Let's say you're busy picking your toes while watching TV—something major like that. Your parents politely ask you not to do it. You overreact and say, "What do you mean I can't pick my toes in the living room? Where do you want me to do it, the garage?"

Then the decibels escalate to the next level. "You know very well why you shouldn't do it. It's gross, it's unsanitary, and if you ever **DO** get married, your wife will throw up the first time she sees you do it."

You respond by turning up the volume another notch. "Oh yeah? Well, with a family like this one, I'll never get married, because I can't stand the thought of having kids and making the same mistakes as you!"

As you can see, **even a pretty minor situation can get out of hand quickly.** In less than a minute you've moved from picking your toes while watching *Earnest Scared Stupid* to promising you'll remain single for the rest of your life.

Hormones.
Puberty.

Since there's nothing you can do to escape the silent alarm clock, you need to be aware of the problems that can come up when it goes off.

There.

You've been warned.

The top ten ways NOT to disagree with your parents.

1. Whine.
2. **Stomp your feet.**
3. Slam your door.
4. Turn your music up **REALLY** loud.
5. Ignore them for three days until they give in.
6. **Refuse to take a shower.**
7. Tell them your other friends have it better than you.
8. When they try to talk to you, turn away and pretend they're not even there.
9. **Squint your eyes and look mean** when they're trying to reason with you.
10. Go ahead and do what you want anyway. It's your life.

The top ten ways TO disagree with your parents.

1. Let them know you understand what they're talking about, repeating back what they've said in your own words.

2. Talk to your parents when they're together. Don't try the old "divide and conquer" scheme.

3. Don't raise your voice.

4. **Fight the urge to throw a teenage tantrum.** That will only convince them their decision was right.

5. Let them know you'll obey their decision, but you'd like another hearing.

6. Thank them for taking the time to reconsider, even if the decision doesn't go in your favor.

7. **Don't retaliate** (or it may be worse the next time).

8. If it turns out that you were right, don't keep reminding them of their mistake.

9. Don't withhold hugs or words of affection. Their love for you hasn't diminished in the least, neither should yours for them.

10. Trust God to work through your parents' decisions.

You can LEARN something from big brothers and sisters.

Older siblings are experiments. That is, your folks didn't know how to parent too well when they had their first child—they had to depend a lot on trial and error. As a result, your older sibling definitely had a harder time than you. The reason: Since he was the first, your parents were probably scared he'd kill or maim himself by making childish mistakes (so they disciplined him diligently). And as new parents, your folks were highly motivated to raise a good kid, one who wouldn't embarrass them in restaurants (so they disciplined him diligently).

The key word here is *diligent.* Parents are always more strict with their first child. That doesn't mean your parents won't be as strict with you, but it probably means you won't be disciplined as often as your big brother or older sister. Believe it or not, parents get tired of being the bad guys all the time. So, by the time other kids come along, they're less likely to put the hammer down. **This can be good . . . and bad.**

It's good because you'll seem to get your way more often. (In reality, your parents have simply learned to better choose their battles.)

And **it's bad** because it will seem as if you get your way more often. You'll be lulled into thinking you deserve to have certain freedoms; then, when your parents finally have to lay down the law, you'll get mad, resent it, or stomp off to your room. Inevitably, that will lead your parents to conclude: "We're not being tough enough, so we better start clamping down more often."

Bad news, right? Many of the freedoms you have built through the years will be curbed until your parents see a change in you. If there's one thing parents don't like, it's having to make a tough decision for their child's welfare, then having that child act like a four-year-old in response to what was probably a very loving thing to do.

So, **how can you learn from older siblings?**

Watch and talk.

Watch what your sibling does to get along with your parents. She might be the type to push your parents to the limit, but more likely she's learned how to read your folks. She knows **when to push and when to back off.**

Talk to her about the battles you think you need to fight. Is it really worth it to throw a fit because you can't stay up until 9:30 on school nights, or should you be obedient during the week in hopes they'll give in to your request for a midnight curfew on Friday?

Obviously, your goal isn't to manipulate or push your folks to always get your way (you're smarter than that, right?). Your goal is to **find out where the guardrails are**—those invisible rules that guide nearly every decision your parents make. Older siblings have probably smashed into the guardrails tons of times. They know how strong they are—and they know where to find the weak spots.

If you want to learn a few things about getting along with your parents, asking advice from the older brothers and sisters in your life is almost always a good idea.

Parents will sometimes EXASPERATE you.

Whenever your parents frustrate you, throw a tantrum, say something mean, and remember their mistake for the rest of your life. Parents are awful people, and all they want to do is make their child's life miserable. **That's the hidden motive of parents everywhere.** They think, *This worthless sapling of a human being has been nothing but trouble and inconvenience since the day he was born. How can I get back at him for all the misery he's caused me?*

Parents not only think that—they act on it. They do everything they can—whenever they can—to get under your skin. **They love it** when you act annoyed, hurt, angry, or frustrated. Watch them walk away after doing something that makes your blood boil. **They smile.** They've succeeded in getting back at you. Your angry response has made their day.

• • • • •

The last two paragraphs are malarkey, of course. They're totally false. We hope you spotted it right away and said to yourself, *What are these nasty sentences doing in this book?*

You say you don't even know what *exasperate* means? Here's a quick definition from *Webster's*: **"To irritate or annoy very much; make angry; vex."**

We know *your* parents never exasperate you—only non-Christian parents have a problem with that, right? Wrong! Otherwise God wouldn't have included this parental "thou shalt not" in the Bible: "Fathers, do not exasperate your children; instead, bring them up in the training and instruction of the Lord" (Ephesians 6:4).

Here are the facts: Parents will exasperate you. Maybe even frustrate you to the point of screaming. **Cut them some slack.** Most of the time it's unintentional; they can't help it. They've got this sin disease that keeps them from knowing the right thing to do in every situation . . . and from doing the right thing even when they know what that right thing is!

Just like you.

Jesus died for your parents' sins, too. They probably don't admit their sins to you very often. (Though, hopefully, they admit them to God quite often.) Let them know you're exasperated, forgive them from your heart (whether they ask for it or not), and remember not to make that same mistake when you're a parent (it's harder than you think!).

Mom and Dad would willingly suffer anything... EXCEPT outliving you.

If you've ever been really sick (the in-the-hospital type) or in a life-threatening situation, and you had the chance to look into the face of your parents, then you know **their worst fear** is something bad happening to you. Losing you will be their big fear the rest of your life.

No parent wants to outlive a child.

Some parents want so badly to see their children live a full and productive life that they go overboard in their parenting—even to the point of not being able to trust God for their children's lives.

When you were little, how many times did you hear, "Watch out for cars!" or "Put that knife down!" or "Does your friend's dad keep any guns at his house?" You may have thought they were being unnecessarily overprotective, but in truth, they could no more **NOT** say those things than your dad can **NOT** clean his plate at dinnertime. It's a physical and emotional impossibility.

Now you're older. You've mastered crossing the street, you don't even think about putting a knife in your ear, and your mom only occasionally asks about guns. **Does that mean they no longer fear something bad happening to you?**

Not even.

Almost every time you go for a drive in a car with a friend, they worry—especially at night or in bad weather. Ditto if *you're* the driver. They stay up until you get home from a date, a basketball game, even a church activity (unless, of course, it's an all-nighter).

Some parents worry more than others. The reason? They know someone or know someone who knows someone who lost a child. Sometimes all it takes is reading an article in the paper or watching a news report about a child dying. Another parent's biggest fear has been realized. TV news shows allow them to see firsthand the grief of another parent. They feel that grief deep down, almost as if it had happened to them. It's a pain unlike any other.

We know having parents that hover or are overprotective can sometimes cramp your style. If you have parents like that, just **give them a big hug** and reassure them you'll be back. You can even remind them that **your life is in God's hands.** Remember, parents can't help worrying about their kids—even just a little.

Stop and smell the PEPPERONI.

Don't be in such a hurry to grow up and move out that you miss the simple pleasures of family life . . . stuff like:

- the smell of frying bacon
- **your mom's chocolate cake**
- the sight of a table piled high with good food
- **the sound of Dad's car entering the driveway for the evening**
- the warmth of sitting in front of the fireplace in winter
- the feel of a freshly ironed shirt
- **munching grilled burgers or hot dogs on the deck**
- the rhythmic sound of the sprinkler in your backyard

Your turn. Go ahead . . . list a few of the little things about your family life that you really enjoy, but tend to take for granted. Our challenge? **Learn to appreciate them!**

____

____

____

____

Use your family to reach your FRIENDS for Christ.

If you have a good relationship with your folks and don't mind being seen with them, God can use you to do amazing things. In fact, He wants to use your family to draw *other* families to Him. Do you realize that **if your friends don't become Christians before they leave high school, there is less than a ten percent chance they ever will?** That means many people who are important to you now will spend eternity separated from the God who loved them enough to die for them. Yes, you should have fun during your teen years, but you also shouldn't ignore the facts.

How can your family help?

• **Make your house the place where people come to hang out.** Create a room that's comfortable and lends itself to good times. Obviously, you have to sell your mom and dad on this idea of reaching out first. If they agree—and if they promise not to try to be best friends with *your* friends—God will do amazing things.

• Find magazines (such as *Brio* and *Breakaway*) and books (maybe Greg's first book *If I Could Ask God One Question* or Susie's book *Guys and a Whole Lot More*) to leave around the house. Let them borrow extra Bibles, Christian music tapes . . . whatever!

• Bone up on the Bible a little. **Refer especially tough questions to your mom or dad.**

• **Suggest your parents invite your friends' parents over.** It could be for a

Super Bowl party, a barbecue, or dessert. This is a must. Why? Well, if a friend does become a Christian, she is going to need her folks to be at least semicomfortable with the idea. Unless they see that your parents are normal people (well, mostly!) they may think their child is interested in a cult.

Relationships help build trust.

It's okay to TALK BACK to your parents.

The trick is doing it *right.* **Here are a few hints:**

- Talk to them the way you want to be talked to.
- Don't raise your voice.
- **Look them in the eye,** but don't glare.
- Give them your attention when they talk to you. Really listen to what your parents are saying. That way, they won't have to ask, "Do you understand what I'm talking about?" (Parents get super frustrated when their children act as though they're ignoring them.)
- Repeat back to them what you hear them saying.
- **Don't whine, nag, or yell "you don't understand."** (They do.)
- Try to wait until everyone's emotions have calmed down. **The worst time to talk** things out is when someone is angry or has had his feelings hurt. Go for a walk first. If you see that a parent is a little huffy, suggest you pick up the discussion later. (But don't say, "When you calm down!" That could just make him angrier.)

The never-ending BATTLE for remote supremacy.

If you're battling over the remote, it's time to call a truce. **It's probably driving your parents crazy!**

Develop a system where at the beginning of each week you decide who gets to watch what when. **Compromise is the key.** By doing this you'll not only escape your parents' anger and get along better with a sibling, you'll improve your **negotiation skills.**

11. Parents get GROUCHY sometimes . . . just like you.

You're probably aware of some of the **pressures** today's parents are under. But if you aren't, here are a few:

- insurance premiums
- increasing taxes
- unfulfilled expectations (in their work and perhaps marriage)
- **leaky faucets** (and other household disasters)
- car problems (car insurance if *you're* driving)
- their aging parents
- wrinkles
- **aches and pains** that didn't used to be there
- pressure to raise their children as Christians in a world that doesn't help.

When parents have a few of these on their minds, and a situation arises with their child, they want to handle things in short order. Decisions that normally would be rationally talked through are made with **lightning speed** (and usually not the way their children want them settled).

You may think your parents are grouchy, but they're just trying to handle things as best they can. Some parents deal with pressures better than others. A key to getting along well at home is understanding what each of your parent's capabilities are—and what level of tolerance each has when the pressure is on. How do you find out? Ask.

"Mom, Dad, when you're under pressure, **what are some things that are difficult for you to deal with?** How will I know when you're feeling the heat?

What can I do to help during those times?"

Your parents are probably able to read your moods like a book. They know when you're under pressure, and hopefully, they know how to treat you during those times. If you don't know the same facts about your folks, find out.

You could save yourself a lot of headaches.

If you hear UNKIND WORDS about yourself—they're not true!

Ever been called an idiot, no-good, lame brain, fat, skinny, ugly, stupid? **Remember this: If God would never use those words to describe you, they're not true. If they're not true, they're lies. If they're lies, don't believe them!**

Some acquaintances, coaches, teachers, brothers and sisters—perhaps even parents—use belittling names to attack you or make you feel bad about who you are and what you can do. We know it's tough to let those lies roll off your back . . . but you must! **Don't believe lies!**

Eight reasons WHY it's not your parents' goal to make your life miserable:

1. If you're miserable, your relatives will notice it when you're together at holiday family gatherings. And your grandparents will wonder how well your parents are doing at parenting. (And knowing Grandpa and Grandma, they'll probably say something.)

2. **They're smarter than they look.**

3. You'll tell your friends, and your folks are concerned about looking cool.

4. They love you!

5. They want you to be a capable adult by the time you hit age eighteen . . . and most capable adults are happy.

6. **They want you to have great memories of your growing-up years.**

7. They don't want you exaggerating things and blowing your homelife out of proportion when you're talking with other adults (such as your youth leader or Sunday school teacher).

8. **They want to make sure you bring their future grandkids to visit so they can spoil them.**

Don't try to CHANGE anyone in your family.

Have you ever wished your little brother would just grow up? Or that your big sister wouldn't treat you the way she does? Or that your parents would just ease up a little on homework?

When someone in your family invades your space or makes your life temporarily miserable (and it will happen), **fight the urge to always wish things were different.**

Here's the deal about change. Sometimes you *can* alter the **outward behavior** of another family member by pleading, fighting, whining, manipulating, ignoring, or threatening. You may get temporary relief if the behavior stops as a result, but it won't last. **Real change takes place from the inside out.** Can *you* change someone from the inside? Nope. Only God can do that. In fact, that's His specialty.

So, if you think you've just got to find some way to change someone living under the same roof as you—**pray for that person instead.** If God wants to change him (and He probably does), He'll do it because of your heartfelt prayers.

Obedience goes a LOOOONG way with Mom and Dad.

You have two choices: (A) Obey. (B) Rebel. What are you going to decide?

Sometimes rebelling *feels* better than obeying, doesn't it? Standing up against authority, looking people in the eye, and saying "no" gives you a feeling of power, of being in control. And it's that feeling of power that sometimes makes you do stupid stuff in front of your folks (or other authority figures).

As a teen, **you want to be your own person and not take orders from anyone else.** The problem is (and you're not going to like this), many teens (not you, of course) aren't wise enough to make their own decisions.

On their third album, *Free at Last,* DC Talk sang a song that said, "Some people got to learn the hard way." The fact is, rebelling isn't the way to go when you're a teen . . . and it isn't the way to go when you're an adult. For ninety-nine percent of us, **there is always someone higher up we have to answer to.** Rebelling against an employer, for example, will just get you fired (which means you won't be able to eat, pay the rent, or date). Rebelling against a college instructor will just get you a failing grade (which means the money you and your parents have soaked into your education will be wasted).

Rebellious behavior never follows through with the rewards it seems to promise. It **ALWAYS** has consequences. Prisons and alcoholic treatment centers are filled with people who thought rebelling against authorities was the way to go. Sadly, they couldn't have been more wrong.

Your parents know this. They also know it's their job to convince you that obedience is the best way. Unfortunately, your parents' methods for getting you to obey aren't always the best. Sometimes their reasons won't seem to be fair or to make sense. It's okay to ask them tough questions when you don't understand. Present your side (calmly—they may change their minds. But just in case they don't, be ready to go along with what they decide). **In the long run, obedience will build your character and give you more freedom** (remember: this is what you really want) than bucking the system.

Let's talk for a second about rebellion from God's perspective. Here's what He says about it: "For rebellion is like the sin of divination, and arrogance like the evil of idolatry" (1 Samuel 15:23a).

The word *divination* can be translated as "witchcraft." What God is saying here is that **rebellion is as great a sin as trying to call up demonic spirits.** In reality, that's exactly what you're doing when you rebel. You're living your life in total defiance of God's rightful authority. This is what Satan wants. He wants you to disobey and ignore every authority God has ordained to protect you. Satan wants you out from under this protection so he can have his way with you.

Are you beginning to see why obedience is so important?

Rebellion doesn't start out full-blown: "I'm going to do drugs, rob a bank, and shoot whoever gets in my way." It starts with small choices to rebel against the authorities God has placed around you to protect you. In time, rebellion becomes a way of life. You live life to do what you want, answering to no one but your own desires.

A lifestyle of rebellion is **big-time trouble.**

Being obedient doesn't make you weak and pathetic; it doesn't mean you shouldn't ever speak up. Obedient people have the maturity to say no to their natural inclination to rebel. **It takes courage to obey.** Obedience shows you're ready to face the world like an adult.

Ten things GIRLS should ask their mom

1. What are some important things I need to look for in a **healthy** relationship?

2. What strengths do you see in me?

3. What weak areas do you notice?

4. What's the secret to having true friends?

5. If I have friends who try to persuade me to do things I shouldn't, **how do I say no?**

6. When I'm out on my own, how do I make my house into a welcoming place?

7. Why does my menstrual cycle affect my moods?

8. How did you know Dad was the right man for you?

9. How will I know God's special plan for my life?

10. What's the most important advice you can give me?

Me? Counsel my PARENTS?!

My (Greg) dad left our home when I was twelve. My mom fell into a severe depression. For two years she drank nearly every night and talked for hours on the phone with girlfriends, trying desperately to make some sense out of her world. She was so despondent that late one night she swallowed a bottle of pills. Fortunately, my sister found her in time.

I remember talking with Mom, encouraging her, and just letting her know I understood. Mom would smile in a way that said, *You're so cute to try and help, I'm glad you're my son . . . but how could you possibly know how to help a woman in her mid-thirties who has never worked a day in her life and has just lost her husband to another woman?* (Pretty revealing smile, huh?)

The truth is, most of the time when parents look at their kids—especially while the kids are young—all they can think about are diapers, pictures on the refrigerator, hours of cartoons, dolls they've played with . . . do you get the picture? They don't see their children as having enough experience to actually help them out when they're going through a tough time.

This means **it's going to be an uphill battle whenever you try to offer advice to parents** (though not necessarily an impossible battle). What you *can* offer—and what they really *need*—is a hug, a prayer, a few words that communicate appreciation for who they are, a look that says, "I will always love you no matter what," an unexpected note, and occasionally, a listening ear. **If God gives you something wise or profound to say, say it.** But don't think you have to fix their problems or teach them how to cope. You probably can't, but God can.

Many parents are a couple YEARS behind.

It's simple arithmetic. **If you're thirteen, your parents will treat you like you're eleven.** If you're fifteen, they'll treat you like a thirteen-year-old. Seventeen . . . fifteen.

Yes, your parents want you to grow up; they just can't believe how fast it's happening. Many would much rather keep you at a nice, safe age . . . you remember, that age when you didn't give them so much grief. (Or do you remember?)

Whether they do it by choice or subconsciously, **gently remind them how old you are.** Reassure your parents that you are the most responsible teenager you know—they've done such an incredible parenting job that **you wouldn't dare think of giving them a hard time.**

Sooner or later, your parents will catch up.

Start a FAMILY NIGHT.

Some of my favorite memories (Susie) of my growing-up years spring from our Friday Family Night. Every Friday after school, Mom and I would get groceries. After we had unpacked and put everything away, our family always went to McDonald's. My brother, Kent, and I could get whatever we wanted. It was great!

Then afterward, **we did something fun together as a family.** Sometimes we went miniature golfing. Sometimes it was bowling, or a trip to the local amusement park. Other times we simply watched TV together, or popped popcorn and played table games. But we were *together.*

What can your family do together? Shop, head to the zoo, have a picnic, make a pizza? Ask your parents if you can designate a "Family Fun Night." Your schedules may be too hectic for a once-a-week event. If so, consider every other week . . . or even once a month. This is a terrific family tradition—one you'll probably want to pass on to *your* kids someday.

Never be EMBARRASSED by your family's lack of something.

Try to see your family as a golden treasure. By the time Carrie learned that lesson, it was almost too late.

Rich in Faith

"Hey, Carrie!" His voice called from the far end of the checkout line.

It was the deep, warm voice of my dreams. But this was no dream. This was a nightmare. **I'd just die if Kevin McKuen saw me using . . .**

"Food stamps." The gum-smacking cashier snapped her fingers in my face. "I need 'em now, honey," she said, blasting out a breath of Bazooka.

I slid them to her, then aimed my grocery cart toward the exit doors.

After loading my sacks in our '71 Nova, I eased onto the sunbaked driver's seat. The crazy old engine jumped and raced, but I finally got it running. Kevin was nowhere in sight. I relaxed my grip on the steering wheel and sighed deeply. **Now if only he hadn't noticed anything strange. . . .**

When I pulled up to our brick duplex, my little sisters mobbed the car. Brenda and Stacy lugged out the brown paper bags while Lindy rummaged through them.

"We've been real good. We haven't even woken Mom up. Did you get us a treat?" Lindy's eyes brightened like a hopeful puppy's.

I scooped her up and propped her against the patched screen door. Hold this open while we get everything inside," I told her. "Then we'll have **POPSICLES!"**

We had just sat down on the back steps with our Popsicles when I heard the telephone. I rushed back in and caught it on the second ring.

"Hello?" I asked, rather breathlessly.

"May I please speak to Carrie?" **It was the voice again.**

My mouth went cottony.

"Carrie?"

I bit off a juicy hunk of my cherry Popsicle and choked it down.

"Hi, Kevin."

"I saw you today at Buy Right," he remarked.

"Yeah?" I wondered what else he saw.

"I was buying the meat for the church Burger Bash. Are you going?"

My heart soared. "I'd like to."

"Do you want a ride?"

"No!" **He couldn't see where I lived.** I searched for a true excuse. "My mom's been sick," I added hastily. "So I might have to watch after my sisters. But if she gets to feeling better, I'll see you there."

I hung up and saw my very pregnant mother in the doorway. Her sweat-drenched hair was plastered to her forehead, and everything about her was swollen.

"Who called?" she groaned.

"Kevin," I said dreamily. "From Highland Estates."

"The redhead who always calls me ma'am?"

"Yes, ma'am." I giggled at my own joke, and Mom's thickened lips formed a slight smile. I gave her an orange Popsicle to keep up the good mood.

"Could you drop me off at the church for a picnic?"

"Why don't you just take the car?" she suggested. "Or ride with Kevin? He lives right up the mountain."

"Mother!" My face flushed. "He'd never relate to our public housing or our junky Bombmobile," I huffed. "I'd rather not go!"

I retreated to my room and fell face down on the bottom bunk bed. **I hated anyone knowing about our tough times.** After praying, I opened my Bible.

"If any of you lacks wisdom, he should ask God. . . ."

I ended up reading the whole book of James. Over and over, God's concern for the poor shouted from the pages. One verse I even underlined: "The brother of humble circumstances ought to take pride in his high position." *Was this the wisdom I needed? If so, I ought to be open with Kevin.*

I tried to imagine his reaction. **Could he possibly understand?** Since Dad walked out on us, we were alone and broke! And Mom's condition kept her from working an outside job. The five of us were barely getting by . . . with the church's gifts and the government programs.

I snapped the Bible shut. No, **I was still too ashamed to tell Kevin,** but I could apologize to Mom.

As I opened my door, I was startled by a painful moan from the den. I ran in and found Mom stretched on the sofa, clawing at her temples.

"Is it the baby?" I screamed.

"No, it's my head." She grimaced. "Get me to the hospital, quick!"

In a matter of minutes we were ready to ride. I jammed the key into the ignition and pumped the gas. It coughed several times, gave a sickly sputter, and died.

I stared helplessly as Mom doubled up. Brenda and Lindy started sobbing.

Stacy draped herself over the car seat and yelled in my ear. "Do something, Carrie!"

So I prayed. *Dear Lord, I need your wisdom. You said if I'd only ask . . .* I didn't have to finish—I'd already heard the answer.

Dashing inside, I dialed the number I knew by heart but had never before called.

"Kevin, I need a ride to Valley Hospital. **Something's wrong with my mother.** We live at the . . . " I took a breath and made myself finish, "housing development right below you—10B."

"Okay." Kevin's voice was steady. "I'll be there in five minutes."

Kevin came in four minutes, along with a pretty girl. "Misti will baby-sit your sisters," he directed. "Let's help your mother into my car."

Neither of us spoke over my mom's agonizing cries. I cradled her shoulders while Kevin concentrated on driving. She was jerking uncontrollably as the EMTs converged on the car and wheeled her away on a stretcher. We tried to follow, but a gray-haired lady stopped us. "I must have some information about the patient," she insisted. I gave her the answers while she keyed them into her computer. **"One last thing,"** she said, eyeing me coolly. "Your manner of payment?"

Glancing sideways at Kevin, I slowly pulled out our Medicaid card, then plopped down to wait on a hard vinyl couch while Kevin paced back and forth. "You can go on to the church now," I said softly. "I'm sorry I ruined your date with that girl."

He stopped dead in his tracks. "What girl?"

"Misti, the gorgeous redhead. Weren't you taking her to the Burger Bash?"

"She's my—"

I raised my eyes and held up my hand to interrupt him. I needed to finish before I lost my nerve. "Does it matter?" I asked. "Now that you know **I'm . . . economically disadvantaged?"**

He laughed.

"You're what? But I thought you were rich!"

I felt my cheeks burning. Not with shame, but with anger. *How could he be sarcastic? Mom and I were doing our best!*

Kevin's eyebrows furrowed at my reaction, then he continued. "Rich in faith. It's a phrase from the book of James."

The verse I'd just read earlier came tumbling out. "Has not God chosen those who are poor in the eyes of the world to be rich in faith. . . ."

Kevin sat down beside me and finished it. "And to inherit the kingdom he promised those who love him?" He looked at me seriously. "Your faith in God is so strong, Carrie. That's what I've always liked about you."

There was no mistaking the admiration in his eyes, and **I was suddenly quite conscious of my appearance:** blotchy face, red Popsicle stains, runny nose. . . . I excused myself for a major scrub job.

When I came back, a young doctor was talking quietly with Kevin. "Mrs. Ward's condition is serious," he said. "She's developed toxemia. Because of her high blood pressure, she's had a seizure."

My lips formed the question **"Alive?"** but no sound came out. The doctor touched my shoulder. "We did an emergency C-section," he explained. "But your mother and little brother made it through fine."

Kevin lifted me up in a crushing hug. **"A new baby!"** he exclaimed.

"Does your mother have a name for him?"

"Randall," I sniffled. "But I've thought of a great middle name." I paused and grinned. "The name 'James' is kind of special to me now. Do you think she'd go for it?

Kevin grabbed my hand. **"Let's go ask her."**

This story by Frances Wildsmith first appeared in the April 1993 issue of Brio *magazine.*

Your parents know what it's like to be a TEENAGER; you know nothing about what it's like to be an ADULT.

We know it's not easy to put yourself "inside your parents' brains." The pressures and demands they're under are tough to relate to.

But your parents HAVE walked a mile in your shoes.

No, not at the same school . . . and in a slightly different era, but their teenage years probably weren't too different from yours.

Ask them if they . . .

- were ever shunned by the popular crowd.
- **were tempted to drink or take drugs or go too far physically with the opposite sex.**
- occasionally cheated on tests.
- dressed in clothes that their parents didn't like.
- watched *Gilligan's Island* or *Brady Bunch* after school instead of doing their chores.
- **were insensitive to their friends** who were going through tough times.

They'll remember doing many of these things. The atmosphere of most junior highs and high schools has changed very little in the last thirty years.

Maybe that's the problem in some homes. The teens know the parents know *exactly* what they're going through—and the teens don't like it. They want to believe their parents don't understand, so they can justify messing up.

But listen: Blaming your parents' lack of understanding of the pressures you're under is never a way to escape taking responsibility for your actions. You'll be better off saying, **"Hey, I'm a teenager. It's my job to make some mistakes, remember?"**

Questions GUYS should ask their moms.

What do girls really appreciate and look for in a guy?

What are some qualities I need to develop before I am ready to date?

When did you begin to notice the difference **between quality guys and average guys?**

What were some cool things dad did while you were dating?

How can I strike up a conversation with a girl without making her think I'm trying to impress her?

How do men earn and keep women's respect?

How is today's dating atmosphere different from when you were dating?

What does mean to be a spiritual leader?

How to have an in-depth CONVERSATION with your parents.

Much of life is routine. Get up, get ready, go to school, come home, do your homework, eat dinner, watch TV, go to bed.

It sounds boring, but that's the way life is sometimes. **What makes life interesting is relationships.**

Relationships take work. You don't develop a close friendship with someone if you never spend time together, right? Good relationships take time—sometimes years—to grow and develop.

We hope it's your goal to have a good relationship with your folks. Since you've stuck with this book this far, you've at least thought about this. But how do you actually do it? Well, part of the solution is just spending time with them. It's next to impossible to be close to people you don't spend time with. Sometimes something incredible happens when you start hanging around your parents: an in-depth conversation breaks out. Suddenly, you are sharing more than just facts.

Here's how to start: ask your parents honest questions, and give them honest answers.

The next reading should give you some good questions to ask your mom and dad. However, asking questions is only half the work. You need to be willing to talk honestly about yourself.

Here are a few things to remember:

- **Let your parents know what you're really thinking, but don't try to shock them.** Saying something you know will raise your parents' blood pressure isn't a good plan. True, you don't want to lie to them, but avoid *deliberately* making them think you're on your way to prison, or hell, or both.

• **Don't simply say what your parents want to hear.** This tactic may bring temporary peace, but it also insults their intelligence. Plus, it does nothing to make the relationship deeper. In the long run, it may even hurt your chances of *ever* being close to them. Parents want to trust what their children tell them.

• **Speak in complete sentences.** Grunts or one-word responses may get your parents out of your face, but they're impolite. Do you want *them* to grunt or give you short answers? Hopefully not!

Not every response has to display your deepest feelings, but some should. If you honestly don't know what you think, say something like, "I'm not trying to get out of answering your question, but honestly, I'm not sure."

• **Give yourself a way out.** It's been said that it's better to keep your mouth closed and be thought a fool, than to open it and remove all doubt. You're entitled to have an opinion, but at the same time you should be able to back up your response. "I'm not sure I know enough to give you a good opinion, but everything I know tells me . . ." This type of response lets your folks know you can think . . . and that you're open to hearing more.

24 Questions you should ask your PARENTS.

• What were the top three "mistakes" your parents made while raising you? Were they really mistakes?

• What are the best memories you have of your parents? The worst?

• If you could give me three character qualities before I graduate from high school, what would they be?

• What does "Well done, good and faithful servant" mean to you?

• How did your parents show you they loved you?

• How would you like me to show you that I love you?

• What about me gives you hope that I'll turn out okay?

• What about me makes you sometimes doubt I'll turn out okay?

• Do you regret the way our relationship is going?

• What do you think of the way I treat you?

• There will probably be times when I disappoint you and let you down. **In what ways do you most want me to succeed?**

Let your dad know how much you APPRECIATE him.

A few years ago, the executives at Hallmark Cards decided to provide free cards to prison inmates around Mother's Day. They even explained that the company would provide postage. **Any inmate who wanted to write a special message on a card and send it to his mom could do so. No charge.**

Inmates loved the idea! In fact, they got so excited about it that **there was almost one hundred percent participation.** Hallmark felt so good about helping to spread goodwill, they decided to repeat the offer for Father's Day.

The same deal applied: Cards and postage would be provided at no cost to every prisoner who wanted to send a greeting to dad.

No one could have predicted it, but *this* time the experiment failed tremendously. Less than one percent of all inmates took advantage of the offer. **Obviously, very few prisoners had a good relationship with their fathers.**

Many times (not always) prisons are filled with inmates who have not had a loving, nurturing, solid relationship with their fathers. And since God intends families to be led by fathers, it's important that we build strong relationships with our dads.

So take a few minutes to think of the things he does that you really appreciate—stuff you usually don't take the time to mention. Write him a note. Give him a hug. **SHOW** him in some way how much you really love him.

Get the most out of family VACATIONS.

Here's what many teenagers think: The older I get, the more time I want to spend with my friends.

That's normal, don't feel bad about it.

Here's what your parents think: The older my children get, the closer they come to leaving home. I don't have many more years left with them, so I should take advantage of the time we do have by spending vacations with them.

Those feelings are normal, too, and parents shouldn't feel bad about them.

Is there a middle ground?

Of course there is! As long as both of you understand where the other is coming from, you can work nearly anything out. Begin by talking to each other in an open and honest way.

YOU

"Dad, the older I get, the less I want to take two-week trips across the country to visit relatives. How would you feel about keeping them to a week from now on? And what do you think about me bringing a friend?"

PARENT

"You'll be leaving home in a few years, and there will be weeks and months at a time where we won't see each other. That's going to be hard for me to handle. I have to admit I'm sometimes a little jealous of your friends because I want to spend time with you without them around. But I see what you're trying to say.

Can you give me some time to think about your request? This business of you growing up is a big challenge."

These changes need to be acknowledged by you *and* your folks. When you discuss vacations, there is usually room for compromise. **Remember: You're not the only one struggling with this growing-up business.**

Now, here are few more vacation pointers:

1. Get involved in the planning, even if it's just for a three-day trip. If you've got a say in the route, what you stop and see, where you eat, etc., you'll have a better time.

2. Keep a journal. Record every detail, including hilarious things people say (waitresses, gas station attendants, little brothers, relatives, strangers at the pool).

3. Be the entertainment coordinator. Think up games or quizzes the whole family can play in the car (i.e., little known geographical details, points of interest, Bible questions, mileage figures, jokes, etc.).

4. Keep a tally of who complains the most. Loser gets cold water thrown in his face at the end of the trip.

And of course:

5. Take lots of pictures.

Ten tips on borrowing MONEY from Dad and Mom.

1. Ask them just after the first or the fifteenth of the month. That's usually the time they get paid. Plan ahead. If you need money for something on the twenty-eighth, ask them on the fifteenth. If you don't, better have your allowance saved. They might be broke.

2. Remember: asking for cash to spend on yourself will be successful maybe only twenty percent of the time. **Be selective about when you ask.**

3. If Mom says no, don't run to ask your dad in the next room. Eventually, he'll find out Mom turned you down. Then the next ten times you want money, he'll remind you of your deception.

4. **Don't make a show of giving money back to God,** but if your parents do accidentally find out that you and a friend are sponsoring a child in a foreign country through Compassion or World Vision, they will be more likely to share their money with you—especially if you are reasonable in your requests.

5. When your parents ask how much money you have, be honest. Tell them the exact amount. To the penny. That will let them know you can be trusted. If they have confidence in you, they are more likely to be generous.

6. **Say please and thank you.**

7. If you need money for a date, ask them for advice about dating before you start talking about "this desperate need you have." Parents like to feel as though they're contributing something more to your social life than fives and tens. (And you just might hear something profound!)

8. When you get home from your date or evening out, give them a report

on how things went . . . then give them the change. Most parents are willing to invest in a quality evening for you and a friend, but they don't want to finance McDonald's for you the next day.

9. If you want to buy a present for your mom, you can ask your dad for as much money as you want. (But you better spend it **ALL** on her!)

10. The more your parents see you waste money on video games, candy, junk food, and other stuff you really don't need, the more likely they are to tell you to start saving your own cash for extra stuff. Since your parents work hard for their cash, they'll feel uncomfortable giving you money when they've seen you consistently blow it.

Prove your growing MATURITY.

Though you may not realize it, parents are always playing the "wait and see" game. They are busy watching your behavior, checking your choices, seeing how you respond in certain circumstances . . . waiting for you to respond to things the way an adult should.

You prove your maturity in two ways: by what you DO and what you SAY.

Guys, if your head constantly turns whenever an attractive girl walks by, or if you're always commenting on the female body, then expect your parents to conclude that you aren't mature enough to date or spend time alone with girls.

Girls, if you spend more time working on your outward appearance than you do on your inward character, expect your folks to encourage you to invest in more spiritual activities. They understand how shallow the world is, how it judges by appearance instead of character, and they know it's nearly impossible to measure up to the world's standard. When you show you're comfortable with who God made you to be and you're not trying to impress anyone but Him, you demonstrate real maturity.

Maturity can't be faked. Sooner or later your true colors will show through. Of course, your parents don't expect you to practice adult behavior all of the time, but they do look for signs of progress. Some examples:

- consistent time alone with God
- intelligent, mature conversation about sex and drugs

- kind remarks toward siblings or people who are getting on your nerves
- **honest questions about how you can reach your friends for Christ**
- taking responsibility for your actions without trying to shift the blame to others
- doing household chores *before* you're asked
- volunteering to do extra things around the house
- making discerning entertainment choices, both at home (with the TV and radio) and when you're out with friends (movies)

Remember: PROGRESS is the key, not PERFECTION!

Clean the bathroom after you've DIRTIED IT.

Why make mom or dad clean up after you? It's time to take a lesson in how to do a good scrub job. Make it one of your weekly priorities. Shower, toilet, floor, sink—it's a fifteen-minute cleaning job—**MAX.**

HONOR and obey your parents.

Ever notice this is the *first* of God's Ten Commandments to end with a promise? Here it is: If you honor and obey your folks, God will bless *you* with a long and fulfilling life! (Sounds good, doesn't it?)

Obedience to parents is so important God not only commands it in the Old Testament, He also emphasizes it in the New Testament. (Check out Ephesians 6:1–3.)

Does God mean we always have to obey our parents? Good question. We're glad you asked. According to James 1:17, God never contradicts himself. "But whatever is good and perfect comes to us from God, the Creator of all light, *and He shines forever without change or shadow*" (TLB, emphasis ours). Clearly, any command from a changeless God should be taken seriously. We ought to honor and obey our folks in every circumstance.

But what if you're being abused? Good point. We believe it's God's will that **NO ONE** be abused. And if you're in this kind of situation, it's not God's desire that you suffer. Even though it's extremely difficult to do, **you MUST tell someone about the abuse.** And not just anyone, either. Seek out an adult—one whom you trust. This might be your pastor, youth leader, school counselor, or even your teacher. **God wants to improve your situation,** but *you* must reveal this painful secret for Him to act through others in your life.

Even in abusive situations, God still wants you to honor your parents by offering them forgiveness for what they have done. Though that may seem impossible now, **He can** fill you with the power you need to forgive.

What if you're from a DIVORCED family?

Unfortunately, I'm (Greg) almost an authority on this one. As I've said, my parents were divorced when I was twelve. Three years later, my mom remarried; this time it only lasted three months. When I was a senior in high school, she remarried again and moved away. I moved in with my dad and his girlfriend (who soon became his third wife). **This is not the way God intended families to be!**

How did I survive? Well, I didn't become a Christian until my freshman year in college, so I didn't have the Lord to turn to. Knowing Him sure would have made those years easier to handle. Since becoming a Christian, I've done a lot of thinking about living in a home affected by divorce. Here are a few things every kid in this situation should consider:

1. Learn from your parents' mistakes. Realize that, more than likely, your parents share the blame for the divorce. When you're old enough to ask the right questions, find out what went wrong in their marriage. Make them be specific about when things started falling apart and why. **Your goal isn't to place blame,** but to make sure you don't repeat their errors.

After living through my parents' divorce, I committed myself to staying married—no matter how tough it gets. No way did I want my kids to experience what I went through!

2. You're going to grow up faster than some of your friends. More will be expected of you at home. The parent you're living with won't always have the time to be there when you have questions or problems, so you'll just have to figure things out as you go along.

Forced maturity is never fun, but it did have one positive result in my case: I learned earlier than I normally would have to face life realistically.

3. Allow divorce to point you to God's way of doing things. After my mom's second divorce, I was extremely angry with God. In fact, since I was going through so much pain, I decided He didn't exist. As a result, for the next three years I lived as if there weren't any God. I did a lot of stupid things and made choices that could have affected me for the rest of my life. (My goal was to try to dull the hurt, but I never succeeded.) Fortunately, God protected me and kept bringing Christians into my life. When I finally turned to Christ, I could see that He hadn't *caused* my parents to mess up; He had only *allowed* it because He loved them enough to give them free will. It was my parents who chose to use their wills to divorce. It wasn't God's fault after all!

Comparing the way my folks did things to God's plan for marriage made me realize that God's way is best.

4. Don't let your parents' breakup harden your heart. The way in which your folks split up (and when) usually determines how bitter you are about it. To protect myself, I unconsciously formed a shell around my heart. That way, I reasoned, I wouldn't get hurt. My shell did protect me, but it also made me a closed person. I didn't let many people inside the real me. When Jesus Christ penetrated that shell, He softened my heart, and it had two immediate benefits:

- **I allowed people to get close** and didn't fear friendship like I did before.

• **I wanted to help others** who were like I used to be—lonely, hardened by the world, lost without hope, and living without a clue.

Entire books have been written on how to survive and thrive with only one parent. **Divorce is not the end of the world,** and many single-parent families are doing surprisingly well. And if my advice here hasn't answered all your questions, talk to someone who can! There *are* answers.

SURPRISE your parents.

Everyone loves fun surprises! Try some of the following, and create more ideas of your own.

- **THANK your mom for dinner** (she'll *love* it!).
- Take out the trash without being asked.
- A couple days ahead of time, tell your mom you're going to make dinner for the family. (Hey, even if it's just cooking some frozen dinners or making sandwiches, she'll **LOVE** not having to be in the kitchen!)
- **Make your own appreciation card** and hide it in your mom's or dad's personal belongings. For instance, sneak it into your dad's briefcase or your mom's purse. Your parent will probably find the card during the middle of a hectic day when he or she most needs a smile.
- Wash the dishes without being asked.
- Bag the leaves from your yard.
- **Wash and wax the family car.**
- Fill your pet's food and water dishes.

Be a BOOK bug.

Yeah, we know you've probably heard a **gazillion times** how important it is to read . . . but here are a few more reasons why reading is smart stuff.

It gives you and your family something to discuss at the dinner table.

It puts you one ahead at book report time.

It sparks your imagination. Creativity breeds creativity, so the more you read, the more ideas you come up with. And the more ideas you have, the more self-motivation you have.

It increases your knowledge.

It broadens your vocabulary. After all, it's not everyone who knows what irpex means.

It makes you sound smart in front of your friends.

It helps your writing. (Really!) If you want to be a good writer, read good writing.

Never LIE to your dad and mom.

Why? Because:

• It's wrong.

• You break one of the Ten Commandments when you lie. ("You shall not give false testimony. . ." Exodus 20:16.)

• You lose your parents' trust.

• When people lie, they often continue to lie to cover up the past lie, and life becomes a vicious circle of lies. (Hey, after the fourteenth lie it's tough to remember what exactly you said two weeks ago that you're still trying to cover up.)

• You could go to jail. (Okay, okay. So we're stretching this a little. Still . . . think about it: Most people behind bars have lied.)

• It's a bad habit to fall into. And once you pick up one bad habit, it's easier to add others. For instance, someone who lies will probably disobey his parents and break curfew and only **PRETEND** to go to piano lessons and forget to feed the pet goldfish (it's not *his* responsibility, is it?). When *that* happens, the fish dies and the kid flushes it down the toilet and buys another one so his parents won't figure out the first one died. But when he doesn't feed the new fish, *it* dies. So he flushes it down the toilet. And this goes on and on and on until the city sewer has an abnormal amount of goldfish floating in the system. And when the evening news picks up the story, his parents casually ask over dinner, "Honey, don't you think it's odd that there are so many dead goldfish in our city's sewage plant?" Since he's fallen into the nasty habit of lying, he'll get really defensive and probably lie again, "Hey! I always wanted a horse anyway. If you'd have just given me a *horse* for Christmas instead of a *fish*, we wouldn't even have this problem. I mean, who could ever flush a horse down the toilet? Not that I know anything about pets going down the toilet . . . but . . . (See what lies get people into? **After a while, nothing makes sense!**)

Even though it may feel like the end of the world when parents separate, there's still HOPE!

Check out the following handles for helping yourself . . . or for understanding what a friend is going through when her family splits.

When a Family Fractures

Dawn whirled around and dialed her dad's telephone number again. Still no answer. He would be thrilled to hear that she won a trophy in the drill-team competition. It was 10:30 at night. *Where was he?*

She remembered the day her dad packed his clothes and left home. "Nothing will change, Dawn," he said. "We'll still see each other all the time." But her dad hadn't even shown up at the competition.

And **everything was changing.** If she and her mom and brother had to move, would she have to change schools? Would they ever have enough money for her to buy anything new?

• • • • •

If your parents are getting divorced, **expect to have jumbled feelings.** One minute you're up, the next you're down. Or maybe you have friends going through this. *Will they ever snap out of it,* you wonder.

Yes, but it will take time. Be patient. If you're the one going through it, sometimes even *you* won't make sense to yourself. You'll want to do things that make a bad situation worse.

YOU FEEL LIKE:
Isolating yourself.

It's tempting to play "lone ranger." You may feel grouchy and figure that nobody wants to be around you because you'll drag them down. If your family's short of money, that makes it hard to be with other teens, too.

Some teens still hang around with their friends, but they isolate themselves *inside.* Dawn did this by adopting a Rambo-woman image. Nothing bothered her. "I'm fine, really," she'd say. As a cheerleader at school, she tried to keep up the same pace of activity as before. It didn't work.

WHAT WILL HELP MOST:
Hang on to your friendships.

Experts say that teens coping with divorce often experience unexplainable headaches, mood swings, or tiredness. If this happens to you, it doesn't mean you're weak, only normal.

If you're afraid you're a drag, say so. Make a joke of it and let your friends tease you about it if it will help.

Stay close to people who love you. Teri says her grandparents, of all people, helped the most. "I could go there whenever I wanted. My grandma makes these great brownies, and we'd sit and talk. My grandparents were always there for me."

Make the best of the money shortage. When everyone's heading out for pizza, suggest an alternative. "I make a mean batch of popcorn, and I think Mom has some ice cream in the freezer. Wanna go to my house instead?"

YOU FEEL LIKE:

Getting your parents' attention by hanging out with rebellious teens.

When Dawn couldn't reach her dad, she thought about those rough older guys who always tried to pick her up after school. *Maybe if I run off with Derrick one night, Mom will call Dad and he'll come get me.* This kind of game doesn't usually work.

WHAT WILL HELP MOST:

Choose friends wisely.

Friends are one of your biggest pluses. People who have a history with you know you. They'll wait for you to bounce back.

YOU FEEL LIKE:

Burying your anger.

If you take your Christianity seriously, you may try to be the "nice" person who only has "nice" feelings. Instead of getting angry, you may even feel like the divorce is somehow your fault.

WHAT WILL HELP MOST:

Don't be too hard on yourself.

If your parents' divorce makes you mad, you're in good company. We'd all like to live like the Brady Bunch . . . but no family is perfect. And kids don't cause divorces—even if the parents say they did. **Parents do the divorcing.**

Find constructive ways to release anger and resentment. The best way is to talk about it with someone who will listen to you without judging. Try your youth pastor, a friend's parent, or an adult friend at church.

Record your feelings in a journal and get them out of your system. Run laps or ride your bike as hard as you need to. Don't be afraid to close your bedroom door and cry. You'll be surprised how much better you'll feel.

If your parents suggest that you go to a counselor, don't say no immediately. Hear the counselor out and think about his or her suggestions when you feel depressed.

YOU FEEL LIKE:

Solving your parents' problems.

You may try to get your parents back together or referee their battles. It's normal to oversimplify other people's problems and think that we can solve them.

WHAT WILL HELP MOST:

Pray for them, but stay out of it.

Marital breakups are complex issues that the two people must be ready to unravel.

If your parents bad-mouth each other, ask them to leave you out of it. Taking sides or getting angry at the "bad parent" can cause you extra grief. If you're curious about what went wrong, ask them in a few years when they have a better perspective.

YOU FEEL LIKE:
Feeling sorry for yourself.

Why not? This will probably be one of the worst times in your life. You look at other families and feel envious. You feel that no one understands how you feel.

Sure, other people in your youth group have parents who are divorced. But now it's *your* parents. You may even feel like a second-class Christian and want to quit going to church.

WHAT WILL HELP MOST:
Take your troubles to God.

God is the only One who *really* knows how you feel. In the dark moments of our lives, it seems we reach out to Him in a new and deeper way. In these rich moments tell Him your troubles . . . even if you're praying the same thing over and over. He never tires of hearing you. Scripture verses that sounded odd before suddenly make sense:

"The Lord is close to the brokenhearted and saves those who are crushed in spirit" (Psalm 34:18).

If your dad is completely out of the picture, that puts you in a special class of people. God provides special protection for the "fatherless" (see Psalm 10:14, 18), and He is there for them: "A father to the fatherless, a defender of widows, is God in His holy dwelling" (Psalm 68:5).

Talk to your pastor, youth leader, or Sunday school teacher about it. Let them reassure you that you're still special in God's eyes.

This article by Jan Johnson first appeared in the March 1992 issue of Brio *magazine.*

Take your parents on a TIME TRIP.

I'm a parent (Greg), and my days are filled with phone calls, writing, driving, appointments, paying bills, helping with homework, attempts at talking with my wife, and a million other things that prevent me from remembering . . . remembering what's going on in my child's world. **I need a reminder.** Your parents probably do, too.

Think back to the last time you were in the middle of a disagreement with your folks. It might have been about curfew, chores, homework, the opposite sex, friends, or freedom. You're making your points, they're making theirs, and no one is budging. If something doesn't give soon, you know who'll win.

When you smack the wall of misunderstanding with your parents, try these terrific tips:

Cool as a cucumber: Stay calm. Yelling won't get you anywhere (except sent to your room).

Do it with diction: Explain clearly and gently how you see the situation.

Reiterate their response: Verbalize the situation as you think your parents see it. (And actually *try* to view it from their angle!)

Query two questions: "When you were my age, did this happen between you and your parents? Do you remember how you felt when you really believed you were right?"

That's all you can do. If you press it beyond this point, you're not handling it maturely, and it's obvious that you simply want your way. Your parents will notice this immediately and will likely dig in their heels.

Do the smart thing: Drop it, and hope things go better the next time.

Here's something to consider when you've done everything you can, but still "lose" an argument with your parents. It's tough for teens to realize, but time and again we've heard stories that go like this: The parent makes what seems to be an "unfair" decision, yet later, it proves to be the right one. You see, somehow God used even their "unreasonableness" to make the right decision. When a final decision *is* made, try to look at it as God's will (because it probably is).

There are things you can't see or know . . . but God can, and He loves you enough to protect you through your parents' decisions.

Before you leave home, learn everything you can about being a HANDYMAN.

Okay, it's true—some dads might need to take lessons from **YOU** on how to be a handyman—but let's assume for a moment that your dad (or maybe your mom) knows his stuff. You'd be smart to take a few weekends out of your busy schedule to ask him to pass along his fix-it secrets. **Just imagine the kinds of problems and tasks you might run up against when you're out on your own:**

- leaky faucets
- **overflowing toilets**
- recaulking the bathtub or shower
- checking car fluids and changing the oil
- fixing a broken or ripped window screen
- **lighting a flare**
- changing a tire
- putting a new light fixture in without electrocuting yourself
- retacking loose carpet
- **programming a VCR** (or maybe you should teach **HIM** this one!)
- successfully putting up a towel rack (you know, without having the screws come out of the wall)
- changing the lawnmower's oil

and of course

- using a saw **without** losing fingers

Establish a family ALTAR.

What is an altar, anyway? Well, in the Old Testament, people often built altars (special places or symbols of their dedication to the Lord) to pray around.

Many churches have altars. And people who attend churches with altars usually like to pray at them. It's nice to have a special place to kneel and talk to the Lord. Of course, you can actually talk to God *anywhere* . . . at any time. You don't have to have an altar to do it. OR . . . **anywhere you pray can become an altar to the Lord.**

When I (Susie) was growing up, my family often had prayer time together. We called this "family altar time." We'd gather in the TV room, kneel, and pray where we were. My dad would get up from his chair, kneel in front of it, and pray for each one of us. Mom would kneel in front of the couch, Kent by the coffee table, and I'd kneel in front of the piano bench (or wherever I was sitting at the time). We'd lift our hearts to Jesus.

It was a close, special time when together we could take our worries and problems to our heavenly Father. I have wonderful memories of our family altar time.

Does your family have a special altar time? If not, why not suggest it to your parents? Ask if there's a night each week when you can all come together, kneel, and pray with one another.

If your parents aren't too keen on the idea, try something like this: "Mom, Dad, every Thursday at 9 P.M., I'm gonna kneel here by our sofa and pray for our family. If you want to join me, great! If not, that's okay, too. I just want you to know that that's what I'll be doing when I'm here every Thursday night. Okay?"

(And when you tell everyone about your altar time, you really have to be consistent in keeping it!) **Can you imagine what the Lord could do in your family after one month of altar time?** There's something humbling about kneeling and praying as a family. Try it!

The rules change a little if you have STEPPARENTS.

If your family is intact, life is simple: your parents make the rules on homework, chores, and curfew, and you obey (after negotiating points of disagreement, of course). But **what if one of the adults in your home isn't your original parent?** Does the Bible's command to honor your father and mother still count? What if your stepparent isn't a believer? What if your "real" parent gives you permission to ignore the stepparent? What if you have only a couple more years before you leave home?

Do you see how complicated it can get? **What's a teen to do?** When dealing with a stepparent, try following these steps:

1. Realize life can hurt. If a parent has died, you'll always feel an empty spot in your heart. No one will fill that special place. More often, though, stepparents enter the picture when one parent decides to divorce the other. Unless the absent parent was abusive, you are left with a void in your family.

2. Talk things through. Before the wedding (or now, if you're already living in a blended family), sit down and talk through the new situation. Try to predict the points of contention that could come up in the next six months (i.e., curfew, who has final say on responsibilities and privileges). Don't talk about solutions until you get all the potential problem areas out in the open.

Then be reasonable. Since everyone's new at this, there has to be a lot of give and take. Don't feel as though everything has to work out exactly like you want it to. That's not going to happen in any family. Your parent and stepparent are still the adults. Hopefully, you can find middle ground on the most important issues.

3. Try to build the relationship. You likely spent hundreds of hours with the previous parent. You hardly know the new one. Start spending time with your stepparent. This may be difficult since you're at an age when time with your parents is already on the decline, but it's a must if you want to build a trusting relationship.

Even if your efforts don't pay off for you, they may pay off for your younger siblings. Your efforts to work at the relationship may show them what to do. If you ignore the stepparent or talk back, thinking you'll soon be out of there, it may cause your siblings to do the same—and they may have to live there for another five to ten years!

4. Suggest regular family meetings. Eventually, your stepparent will do something to make you mad. How are you going to react? Throw a fit and ignore him for six months? Or will you take the mature approach and talk it over?

Mistakes are inevitable. Recognize that and make an effort to keep talking. Talking is better than silence. If your stepparent doesn't make an effort to fix the situation, there might not be anything you can do. At the very least, don't be the problem. Be the one who always pursues the right solutions (read Romans 12:18).

So what about obeying stepparents? Even though there's no specific biblical command to obey stepparents, it's a safe guess God wants you to. (Susie says: Unless they ask you to do something illegal or immoral . . . like taking money from the church offering plate to buy twelve pounds of bubble gum.)

What if the parent who no longer lives with you tells you to ignore your new parent? Do the right thing: Help the parent whose roof you're under. Your mom or dad is trying to start a new life and create some sense of normalcy. Your parent has likely been hurt just as you have. Try not to make the hurt any worse.

What if the stepparent isn't nice or doesn't seem to care about you? Take the high road. Pray for him and look for ways to be nice.

We realize this short chapter hasn't covered everything there is to know about living in a blended family. There are whole books on this subject you may want to check in to at your Christian bookstore. But if you keep a positive, Christian attitude and do all you can to make the situation work (pray!), it usually will. Really.

Be grateful for your ALLOWANCE.

Some teens don't even *get* an allowance. And yeah, we know, some teens get a lot more than you do! But if you learn how to handle money wisely, you can stretch your money.

Numero Uno Important Thang: No matter how much or how little money you receive, **always tithe at least ten percent.** God commands us to do this. If we refuse, **we're actually stealing** from our heavenly Father. *Yikes!* After all, everything we have already belongs to the Lord. He **COULD** ask for sixty-five percent—but He's only asking for ten. If you take Christianity seriously, tithing really isn't an option.

Numero Dos Important Thang: Always save ten percent. My dad (Susie) taught my brother and me these two important facts about money during our years at home. He believed if we always tithed and saved, we'd usually have enough money for what we needed.

Our family was never rich—both my parents were schoolteachers—but we always had enough . . . and a little left over. And *I* believe it was because we were faithful to God *and* faithful to save.

YOU try it!

Remember your goals: INDEPENDENCE from your parents and DEPENDENCE on God.

You won't wake up one morning having both; it's a gradual process.

Have you ever been to a wedding? The father of the bride marches his beautiful daughter down the aisle to the man who will pledge to take care of her the rest of their lives. Often, the minister asks the father, "Who gives this woman to be married to this man?" The father replies, "Her mother and I." After he's said that, he takes his daughter's hand and places it in her husband-to-be's hand.

In a slightly different way, that's what your parents are supposed to do with you. **They are supposed to take your hand from theirs and place it in God's.**

As you're going through the years-long process of breaking away from your parents and learning how to be a responsible adult, you need to reach out to the Lord and take a tighter grip of His hand. If you're not doing that, it will be tougher for your parents to let go, because they will know that you aren't spiritually ready to go out into the world.

So go ahead, break away from your parents; become more independent. But **while you're at it, reach out and grab the Lord Jesus Christ with both hands . . .** and hold Him tight. When you do, you will be completing the great quest your parents and you have been on for eighteen-plus years. It's a quest with heavenly and earthly rewards. But if you refuse to reach out to God, there will ultimately be no reward for you.

More independence from parents means more dependence on Him. Deal?

Feed and water your PET.

(If you don't have a pet, feed and water your little sister, your stuffed animals, or the kid down the street.)

When you were in grade school, you probably begged your folks for an animal. Why did they give in? Because you promised a **million times** that you'd take care of it. Well, have you kept your promise?

This probably isn't an issue that parents will get hugely upset about if you don't follow through now that you're an ultrabusy teen. But . . . hey, a promise is a promise.

Fulfill your responsibility—take care of your pet.

Be POSITIVE!

If you *really* try, **you can find something positive to say about everything.** And that's important. Know why? Because a positive attitude helps create a positive atmosphere. Go ahead, try it! Strive to think of something positive to say. **Here are a few ideas to get you started:**

- "Mom, this zucchini and prune salad is certainly a unique creation! And I'll bet it's pretty healthy, too, huh?"
- "Dad, thanks for taking me to school in your exterminator's vehicle. I didn't have *one* bug crawling on me the entire day!"
- **"I know these accordion lessons are gonna come in handy someday!** If not, at least my patience has grown."

Give Mom and Dad a chance to DATE again.

Believe it or not, **your parents had a life before you were born.** They dated, spent romantic moments together, talked without interruption . . . they loved spending time alone with each other. Then they decided to become parents, to unselfishly give their love to another human being for the next twenty years of their lives. They couldn't predict all the consequences of that decision, but like many couples, the price they paid was time alone together.

Some marriages never recover from those years of neglecting each other. **When couples are in their second decade together** (like your parents probably are), **it's easy to get into a rut.** They build a habit of not spending time with each other, and their children keep them too busy to date and romance like they used to. None of this, of course, is your fault. When you were younger, there was nothing you could do about it. Now you can.

If you're the oldest and there are smaller siblings at home, tell your parents you'll baby-sit for them one evening every two weeks or so. **They REALLY need that time alone together.** My (Greg's) parents divorced when I was twelve. Part of the reason, I believe, is they quit investing in their marriage when we kids were little. They were so busy taking us everywhere, they didn't make time for each other. My wife's parents divorced after twenty-five years, too. Again, neglecting the relationship was the culprit.

If you already live in a single-parent family, there's certainly nothing you can do about it now (and remember, it wasn't your fault). But if you do live in a two-parent family and want your parents to stay together, then **give their**

relationship a boost. Here are a few lines to try:

"Go for a walk, I'm fine."

"Why don't you farm us kids out to friends for the weekend so you can have some time alone?"

"Isn't it about time you guys had a second honeymoon? What can I do to help arrange it?"

"Dad, do something special for Mom this Valentine's Day besides buy her a card."

Be persistent and pray. You could even go to a Christian bookstore and buy your parents a book on dating ideas for couples. Hopefully, they'll take the hint.

Age does NOT determine when you're ready to drive.

Fifteen . . . learner's permit, sixteen . . . license. Period. No discussion. That's how it's always been and how it always will be.

For some teens, maybe. For others, it might be a death sentence. The driving privilege is a lot like a later curfew. **Maturity should be the determining factor, not age.** Parents who care, realize this and will make sure of two things:

1. You won't be able to take a car out by yourself until you've shown a high level of maturity and responsibility (as well as proficiency at driving, of course).

2. If you fail to maintain a certain level of cooperation around the house and maturity in your behavior, the car will be the first thing to go.

If you have access to a car, you know that wheels mean freedom. **Do you want your freedom?** Then choose to be **responsible** with homework, chores, curfew, and how you treat your folks. When you choose to be mature, you show you are ready for a license.

LEARN from your parents.

Think about it. Your parents have lived a **LOT** longer than *you* have, and they've picked up a ton of information along the way. If you practice these two tips, you'll be surprised at what you can learn!

Be observant. What do your parents do well? Your mom's a good cook? Great! Act like a sponge and soak in as much as you can by watching her. Michelle learned how to debone a chicken by watching her mom do it. Geoff learned how to change a flat tire by hanging around his dad. Ashley learned how to decorate cakes by watching her mom do it every week for their family's small business.

You'll be surprised at what you can learn just by keeping your eyes open!

Ask questions. If your mom or dad does something you don't understand, ask about it! This is one of the best ways in the world to learn. After pulling his jeans out of the washer, Mark's mom always hung them up to dry instead of putting them in the dryer. One day he finally asked her why she did this, and he found out it kept his jeans from shrinking. So when he left for college—where he had to do his *own* washing and drying—that tip came in real handy!

Hugs go a LOOOONG way!

It sure feels GOOD to be hugged, doesn't it? Why not spread some of those great feelings to your family? Think about it. When was the last time you hugged your brother or sister? **Try it!**

We all like to be touched by someone we love. So why not give Dad a good ol' back rub? Squeeze Mom around the shoulders and give her a smile. You'll not only make your family feel better . . . **but you'll feel better, too.** We promise!

If you're going to be late, CALL.

When you were little, you had an incredible imagination (perhaps you still do). You just knew there were monsters in the closet and dozens of ten-foot-long poisonous snakes underneath your bed. If the room was dark, something just *had* to be walking around inches from your bed. A creature so hideous, it could eat you in one bite . . . but you'd be in pain for the next one hundred years.

Of course, your parents came to the rescue whenever you called. They left the hall light on all night so you wouldn't get scared. They even came in and chased the monsters away. They rocked you and sang you to sleep. They prayed away the fears until you realized that God was always with you, taking care of you.

When you became a teenager and started to want to spend more time with friends, your incredible imagination was somehow magically transferred to your parents. With one major difference: **their imagination goes crazy only when you're away from home.**

If you're five minutes late, your parents are fine. Ten, they're checking their watch and looking out the window every twenty seconds. Twenty minutes late and they're calling your friend's parents. At thirty, they're scared and angry all at the same time. And if you're forty minutes late, they are ninety-five percent convinced you're in a hospital emergency room with your intestines hanging out on the operating table. All those years of piano lessons, down the tube.

There's one simple way to banish their fears: a phone call.

"Lost track of time, Mom, but we're on our way. Everyone's sober and I'll be home in seven minutes and thirty-three seconds."

Your parents relax—they can breath easy. And so can you (now you won't be grounded for the next two months).

TOP TEN nice things you can do for your dad.

1. Hug him and let him know you think he's great.

2. Fix up his work bench.

3. Pull weeds, rake leaves, sweep the garage . . . **make his load lighter by taking over any chore he usually does.**

4. Treat his wife (your mom) with respect.

5. Don't act as though you're ashamed to be around him when you're with your friends. You could even brag about him in front of them when he's in earshot.

6. **Take him out to Denny's for pie and coffee—your treat.**

7. Suggest you two start doing something fun together: golf, tennis, racquetball, cribbage, backgammon, chess, shopping, talking before bed, walking, hiking, fishing . . . whatever. Just do something together you both would look forward to.

8. **Talk about the really important stuff he's taught you.** It can be something about life (staying a virgin until marriage), or just horse sense (never honking your horn when you pass a group of Hell's Angels on the freeway).

9. Write him a letter at least once a year letting him know how much you appreciate him. Be specific.

10. Pray that he will always keep his promises to God, others, and himself.

COMPROMISE is the name of the game.

Unfortunately, it's not always a game parents (or teens) like to play. The reason? Their parents probably didn't play it with them.

Your parents had to grin and bear it when they were teens, and they figure since they lived through it, you will too. Besides, some believe the universal scales of justice are simply evening out. They lost so many disagreements when they were teens, it's time now for them to win a few. They've got the power, they've got the car keys, they've got the cash . . . hey, it's their turn to do the touchdown dance!

But let's assume your parents want to play another game: they want to keep their teens on their team. That means doing a little give-and-take. You give your side, they'll give theirs. Hopefully, you can meet someplace in the middle.

Compromise can be great. Suggest your parents try it with you. You won't regret it.

You won't know how much your parents LOVE you until you're a parent.

Have you ever been taken for granted? Of course you have! How about for twenty-five years? Probably not.

The last thing on your mind right now is raising children, right? You've got too many other things to worry about: tests, the opposite sex, sports, friends, the opposite sex, college, becoming more independent, the opposite sex . . . Who has time to worry about kids?

Maybe you've heard this from your parents before, but **raising kids takes work.** Heavy-duty sacrifices of time and money. Your parents *used* to invest those things in themselves; now they take what little time and extra cash they have and pour them into you.

Two things should come to mind when you consider this:

1. Am I worth the investment? Are you turning into a young man or woman who puts something back into others, or are you ungrateful, thinking only of yourself?

2. Have I told my parents I appreciate what they've done? Maybe you have, but probably not too often. Most of the time, that's okay. Most parents aren't expecting you to write syrupy letters once a week in praise of all their unselfish sacrifices.

But how about once or twice a year?

Most parents don't want much . . . just a healthy child who does her best in school and isn't self-destructive (drinking, drugs, etc.). If they get a grateful child, that's just gravy.

Nearly all parents we've ever talked to say they wouldn't trade their children for

the world; they'd gladly die for them, and are willing to do whatever it takes to provide for their needs.

Don't wait until you're twenty-five and a parent to realize what your parents have done and are doing for you. Pass them some gravy once in a while. They'll love it!

TOP TEN nice things you can do for brothers or sisters.

1. Fold their clothes.

2. **Volunteer to do one of the chores they hate doing.**

3. Put toothpaste on their toothbrushes so all they have to do is walk in the bathroom and start brushing.

4. Remember special occasions: birthdays, Christmas, graduations, spiritual birthdays, Arbor Day, etc.

5. Leave them notes describing something you admire about them. (I saw you reading your Bible last weekend. I'm glad I have a sister who knows what's important in life.)

6. Let them know you're praying for them when they are going through finals or have a term paper.

7. Go to as many sports events as you can, cheer them on, then comment about their specific accomplishments. ("You didn't kick the coach in the knee when he didn't put you in until the last thirty seconds of the game. That must have taken a lot of self-control!")

8. Wander (invited) into their rooms and **strike up a conversation.** They might need to talk to you about something, but think you're too busy to bother.

9. Play a game with them when they're bored.

10. **Give them something of yours that means a lot to you.**

Honest humility goes a LOOOONG way.

I (Greg) was thirteen, and it was a very difficult time in my life. It was just me, my mom, and my older sister at home. Mom was working full time, and my sister had several full-time boyfriends. As for me, I was feeling pretty neglected. One night I unloaded on my mom about all the things I wasn't getting or couldn't do. She listened, and then, in a not-so-patient tone, detailed several things she **HAD** done for me.

I was stunned. Mom was right. My life wasn't so bad after all. She *had* been doing her best and . . . and given the circumstances, she'd done a pretty good job.

I felt bad. I apologized in a very puppy-dog tone. I had to repeat my apology a number of times before she realized it was genuine, but she finally forgave me.

Apologizing to parents isn't easy. You hate it when they're right. **YOU** want to be right once in a while and make **THEM** say they're sorry. But it's usually the other way around.

My mom had a tough time forgiving me (outwardly, anyway). Here she was doing her best to make a normal life of things, and there I was telling her how badly she was failing. I had been ungrateful. The only thing that could make up for it was humility.

True repentance, the kind where you look a parent in the eye and admit you're wrong, **will ALWAYS go a long way.** Not only will it allow you to move on from a dumb mistake, but it's good practice for the future. And since you'll probably be making dumb mistakes the rest of your life (at work, with your husband or wife, with *your* children), humility is a quality of character you must develop.

Have you ever met someone who couldn't admit she was wrong? Do you like spending time with that person?

Nuff said. Probably want to pass it on to *your* kids someday.

Help your parents to be ENCOURAGERS.

Barry is a sixteen-year-old guy with good looks and a great sense of humor. Even though his entire family is active in our church, Barry's dad sticks out—in the wrong way. You see, he's sarcastic. **VERY** sarcastic. And coarse. He tells rude jokes and sometimes makes offensive remarks. *He* thinks he's funny—but he's not.

Barry is beginning to echo many of his father's habits. Though it's natural to imitate the people we're around the most, it can have sad results—especially if our role models are not Christlike. Chances are Barry will turn out exactly like his dad—unless he consciously chooses a different lifestyle.

It will be tough, but Barry can help his dad to change by encouraging him to build up family members instead of putting them down. Here are a few suggestions for how to pull it off:

- **Don't try to correct your parent.** Many times a parent like Barry's dad acts the way he does simply to get attention. If Barry corrects him, it won't change this craving. Chances are, his father will respond in anger.
- **Praise your parent when he or she DOES act in a positive manner.** Barry needs to be on the lookout for times when his dad **ISN'T** being sarcastic. If Barry can find things he really **LIKES** about his dad and begin pointing them out, his father may not feel such a need for constant attention.

This strategy can also work for a parent who often complains or puts you down. Overcome negatives with positives whenever possible.

Genuine compliments go a LOOOONG way.

Some examples to get you started:

"I don't say this too often, Dad, but I'm very thankful I have a father who has **done such an excellent job** providing for his family—both love and the things we need."

"Mom, I appreciate the fact that you were willing to go back to work so I could go to college."

"Did I ever thank you for folding my clothes for twelve years before I finally caught on—with your help—that **this was something I could do?** No? Well, thanks."

"I realize an allowance is a gift and not an right. **Thanks, Mom and Dad, for that weekly gift. I'll try not to waste it."**

Try to see your brother or sister as a real HUMAN BEING—instead of someone who was created just to make your life miserable.

My Brother/My Friend

For years I thought he was an alien from another galaxy . . . until that special night.

MICHAEL: Hey, Blondie, I'm still hungry. Wanna go get a milk shake?

MANDY: You buying?

MICHAEL: Why? Don't you have money?

MANDY: Yeah, I do.

MICHAEL: Really?

MANDY: Yeah.

MICHAEL: Can I have some?

MANDY: In your dreams!

MICHAEL: Get your shoes on and meet me in the Jeep.

I put that conversation in my journal, for the record.

Why, you ask?

Because **it may be one of the most significant dialogues in American history**—right up there with the Clinton-Bush-Perot debates.

Because it took place between two people who just a few months before were still calling each other Pizza Face and Miss Piggy and preferring not to be seen in the same room, car, or restaurant booth by their respective friends.

Because that conversation took place between me and my brother.

It was so weird.

Ever since I could remember, Michael and I had been fighting—over who had a bigger piece of cake or who got to ride in the front seat on a three-block ride to the grocery store. We couldn't even sit down to watch TV without battling over what show to watch or who was going to hold the remote control.

"You two used to play so cute together when you were little," Mom said to us one day when Michael was snapping me with a towel during a dish-washing session.

"You got us confused with somebody else's kids, Mom," Michael said.

"I wish you *were* somebody else's kid," I muttered.

"I think you *are* somebody else's kid," he muttered back.

SOMEONE PINCH ME: AM I AWAKE?

That may not seem weird. **THIS** is what's weird. When I started high school, two years behind Michael, things gradually changed. It began when I brought home my class schedule the first day. He was in the kitchen, foraging, and I went in to catch any crumbs that might be left over.

"Who do you have for geometry?" he said.

Dazed, I looked around the kitchen. "Who . . . *me?*" I said.

"I don't see anybody *else* in here."

"Cranston," I said.

"No way! Get out of that class or you'll never see the light of day until after the final."

"But I can't get a schedule change now! They said—"

"Forget 'they.' There are ways. I'll get you out of there. Who've you got for English?"

"Getz."

"Cool. Biology?"

It wasn't until later that I realized we'd gotten through an entire conversation without snarling. I didn't even slam my door when I went to my room.

I thought at first it was just a mental lapse he'd had—that maybe he mistook me for some stranger passing through the kitchen. But that wasn't the end of it.

The next week he got his license, and naturally he looked for every excuse to drive the car. Mom caught on fast that he could now do taxi duty, and he started carting me to gymnastics and choir practice and Liz's house. He didn't complain—I mean, it got him behind the wheel.

During those rides, he started coaching me on how to get through Getz's essay tests and teaching me what the clutch was for. It was during those rides that we started calling each other Bro and Blondie instead of Pizza Face and Miss Piggy.

Now, mind you, we weren't making pacts to name our firstborn after each other or anything. But I was convinced that if my skin accidentally touched his, he wasn't going to scream and run for the cootie-killing spray. It was obvious he thought I was OK. And then that one Friday night I was really convinced.

HEART TO HEART

It was Michael's first weekend night to take the car out. He was supposed to be in by 11 P.M. He called at 11:15.

"Flat tire," I heard Dad say when he hung up the phone. "I tried that story when I was sixteen. Does he think we're stupid?"

"I think *lame* is the word they use now," Mom said.

It occurred to me that maybe Michael *did* have a flat tire. It didn't occur to our parents until he came home and found he had to convince them by pointing out the spare on the right rear and the flat in the trunk.

"Oh, okay," Dad said. "It's late. Let's go to bed." Michael was the first one to go—and he slammed his door. I didn't blame him for his anger. Around midnight, I heard him come out of his room, and I followed him into the kitchen. Michael always grazed when he was upset.

"He could have at least apologized for not believing you," I said, handing him the peanut butter he couldn't locate because males can never move anything to find what they want.

"No doubt. It's like they raise this good Christian son, then look for reasons not to trust him. Why is there never anything to eat in this house?"

"Because *you* live here," I said. "There's cold pizza in the meat drawer."

"How come you always know this stuff?"

"I'm female."

He looked at me for a minute as if he'd never considered that fact before. Then he plopped a plate of Mom's homemade pizza on the snack bar and dragged the stool up to it.

"Want some, Blondie?" he said.

"Sure. I love acid indigestion."

"I'll split a bottle of Pepto-Bismol with you later."

From there on, it was . . . how do I describe it? A special night.

We talked about everything—how glad we were that Mom and Dad had raised us to be Christians and what had made us each commit our lives to Christ. We shared bummer stories about kids putting us down because we didn't swear and pressuring us to go to drinking parties. By the time we'd gotten the pizza down to crusts, we'd even told each other how we prayed.

"You know what's cool?" he said.

"What?"

"We used to hate each other. Now we actually pray to the same God."

I was awake a long time that night. I couldn't go to sleep until I finally put something together: If you share the most secret part of yourself with a friend, you get a little nagging doubt later because you're afraid she might tell somebody else. But **when your friend is your brother,** you don't have that, because **you know you can trust him.** He's family.

"Night, Blondie," he said outside my door.

"Night, Bro," I said.

After that I started writing in my journal the stuff we talked about in the car—just for the record—like jokes we had . . . even whole conversations. It was as though I had this whole new friend.

HEY! WHAT HAPPENED?

And then Tuesday afternoon happened. About 3:30 I went into the kitchen to empty the dishwasher and found Michael in there with two of his basketball buddies, Jason and Scott. They were sitting at the snack bar practically salivating, and Michael was pulling open drawers and slamming cabinet doors.

"Do you have a search warrant?" I said.

"I smell brownies. I know Mom made brownies."

"Mom and Dad are gone until after dinner," I said. "She made us a casserole *and* brownies."

"Where are they?"

I lifted the lid to the cookie jar and pointed in.

"Thanks, Miss P.," he said, then pinched my cheek. Pinched my cheek. I stared at him as he tucked the cookie jar under his arm and plopped down at the snack bar with it. **I should have known what was coming.**

"We got any milk?" he said, his mouth crammed with brownie.

The hair started standing up on the back of my neck. "Try the refrigerator," I said.

"Hey, she's pretty good," Scott said.

Michael gave me a drop-dead look and said, "She *thinks* she's good."

I wasn't sure what was going on, and I'm sure my face showed it. I turned my back on him and started yanking glasses out of the dishwasher.

"You're a freshman?" someone said behind me.

"Unfortunately," I said.

"I thought Michael was lying. You don't look like a freshman."

"Give her time, man. She'll catch up," Michael said, staring intently at the milk he was pouring. **"She hasn't lost all her baby fat yet."**

Before I could hurl a stack of plates at him, Jason said, "No—I mean, you look older than that. I saw you working out with the J.V. girls' basketball team the other day, and I went, *Whoa, what's that junior doing with all those freshmen?*

Michael proceeded to choke on a brownie and lunged for his milk glass. I tried to kill him with one piercing glare, but he kept gasping for air.

"Really! You're pretty good," Jason said to me. "You oughta come shoot some baskets with us."

Michael made a miraculous recovery and yelled, "Not!"

"You afraid she'll make you look bad?" Scott said.

"Nah. I'm afraid we'll hurt her." Michael held out his empty glass to me. "Why don't you put this in the dishwasher before you run on along, huh?"

WHO IS THIS GUY?

I didn't "run on along." In fact, I was pretty proud of the exit I made. I smiled sweetly at them all—except for Michael, at whom I curled my upper lip—and then I swept from the kitchen with the cookie jar in hand.

What I really *wanted* to do was dump the whole thing over Michael's head and yell, **"Eat them all, Pizza Face! I hope you turn into one big zit!"**

By the time I got to my room—and slammed the door—every inch of me was stinging. I'd played Michael's game and maybe even won. But the fact that he'd started it to begin with hurt me inside and out. I whipped out my journal and started scribbling.

"So much for our 'friendship,' Brother," I scrawled. That was as far as I got. I wanted to go on with, "I hate him. I *hate* him. **He made me look like a fool in front of his friends just when I thought I could trust him to treat me like a person.** He made me think I *could* trust him—and I can't—and I hate him!"

But I couldn't write it, because I didn't hate him. I loved him. In the last couple of weeks I'd really started to figure out who he was, and I liked what I was finding out. I wanted the relationship with him that he'd shown me we could have, and now he was playing around with it like one of his stupid basketballs.

I tossed my pen across the room. Maybe my parents were right. You could raise this good Christian son, but you really couldn't trust him to behave like one.

I pulled a brownie out of the cookie jar, but before I could stuff it in my mouth, I stopped. And what about me? What about that sweet exit I'd just made from the kitchen? Was I any better? Now what? Was I going to sit around and wait for him to make the next move? **Or was I going to make like a Christian and love instead of hate?**

I hate to admit it, but just then I wasn't sure. I didn't find out myself until later.

TRUE CONFESSIONS

Around 6 P.M. I heard Michael alone in the kitchen. He must have opened and closed the refrigerator door five times without taking anything out.

My mind was saying, "I hope you starve," but my feet took me out to the kitchen, where I opened the door to the fridge, moved the milk carton, found the casserole, and popped it into the microwave. I moved like a robot, and Michael wasn't much looser. He stood in the middle of the kitchen and mumbled, "Will we need ketchup for that?"

"I would assume so," I said, my voice chilly. "You put ketchup on just about everything, don't you?"

He made one attempt to locate the bottle and then barked, "Well, where in the world *is* it?"

That's when I knew what I was going to do. I turned around and plastered myself against the pantry door. "It's in here," I said. "But you're not getting it until you **answer a question for me,** so unless you want to starve, you'd better be honest."

He rolled his eyes and plunked himself down at the snack bar.

"Why would you start a really good friendship with somebody and then turn on her?" I said. "You know, make her look stupid in front of people, that kind of thing?"

Michael lifted his lip. "I wouldn't. I would never do that! Ask any of my friends."

With a leap I left the pantry and whirled to face my reflection in the oven door. "Mandy," I said to it, "you're one of Michael's friends—or at least I *thought* you were. Has he ever done that to you?" I put both hands up to my face.

"Why, yes, as a matter of fact just today he made a total fool out of me in front of two guys. All this time he's been treating me like a real person, but he doesn't seem to want his friends to know that. After all—I'm his little sister—gross!"

"Oh, come on, Mandy!" Michael said. "I was with my . . . it's a whole different thing."

I spun around to face him. "Michael, I wasn't going to horn in on your whole afternoon. I'm not interested in going out and shooting baskets with you. And even if I were, did you really think I was going to stand there and whine because you guys wouldn't give me the ball?" I came toward him at the snack bar and slapped my hands on the counter. **"I just wanted to be treated with respect,** because that's what I've learned to show you. **And it has to be all the time—not just when nobody else is looking."**

The microwave dinged, and I flung it open. "Stir it and put it in for three more minutes on high," I said as I headed for the door. "I'm not hungry anymore."

"Hey—" he said.

"The ketchup's in the pantry!"

"No—Mandy—wait!"

I stopped, but I didn't turn around.

"Look," he said behind me. "I know I was a jerk. I knew it when I was doing it . . . and I'm sorry. It's just—**I thought you'd think you were supposed to hang around with me all the time or something."**

I looked at him then, and I just shook my head. "It's kind of like a friend of mine once said. Why would you raise this cool sister, and then look for reasons not to trust that she would always be cool?"

THIS IS WHAT FRIENDSHIP'S ALL ABOUT

When I got to my room I didn't slam the door, so it was still open when about an hour later Michael poked his head in.

"Hey, Blondie, I'm still hungry," he said. "Wanna go get a milk shake?"

"You buying?" I said.

"Why? Don't you have money?"

"Sure I do."

"Really?"

"Yeah," I said.

He looked at me innocently. "Can I have some?"

I snorted and threw a pillow at him. "In your dreams!"

A grin broke over his face as he tossed it back. "Get your shoes on and meet me in the Jeep."

He gave me a look then—a look that said *I'm sorry and I love you and I respect you and* **I'm glad you're my kid sister.**

I couldn't record *that* in my journal. So I just kept it in my heart.

This story by Nancy N. Rue first appeared in the November 1994 issue of Brio *magazine.*

All parents have a few basic PROBLEMS.

Contrary to childhood perceptions, **parents aren't perfect.** The big difference between them and you is they've learned to hide their imperfections better than you. They've probably also learned from their mistakes and are making fewer of the same ones. That's why they might still seem a bit more perfect than you. But they're really not, and here's why:

- **They are sinners.** Your parents want to be perfect, but they aren't. Only the death and resurrection of Jesus Christ can take away their sin. They're just like you.
- **Your parents had parents.** Often, grandpas and grandmas made even worse mistakes parenting your parents than your parents are making with you. Their folks could have been the "silent type" who didn't talk about their feelings much. They just quietly did their work, raised their families, and lived a normal life. That could be a reason why your mom or dad doesn't talk about deeper things with you.

Perhaps their parents were abusive because of alcohol or drugs or a personality that was just plain ornery. If your grandparents weren't Christians, your folks likely have a lot more to overcome than they would if they had been raised by consistent Christian role models.

- **The world is more dangerous than it used to be.** Your folks are probably a little more scared, more on edge than their parents were. The news media constantly reports on drive-by shootings of innocent victims, rapes, drunk drivers killing carloads of fun-loving high-schoolers on their way home from football games . . . **we're not in Kansas anymore, Toto.** Nope, we're in good ol' North America. The land of the free and home to a lot of crazy and dangerous people. So . . . cut them some slack if they're acting overprotective. They can't help it!

- **They're twenty-two-year-olds trapped inside thirty- or forty-something bodies.** Behind those emerging wrinkles lies the heart of a young adult. They're not even close to being ready for the old-folks home. How can you tell? Their hearts still want to do crazy things and they're only now realizing their bodies are rebelling. *Hey, cut that out. You can't play tackle football anymore or that muscle is going to pull right off the bone!*
- **They're tired.** But you already know that, huh?

So the next time you think you're the only one who has problems, sit back and observe your folks for a day or two. Your problems just might fade into oblivion.

ALWAYS eat what your mom makes for dinner.

Yep, even if it's something you don't really like. **Try to put yourself in her shoes. She's tired and she has a lot on her mind.** Probably the last thing she wants to do is make dinner for the family. But she does . . . because she loves you. And she cares about what you eat.

So when she does serve eggplant and liver casserole and you don't like it . . . **eat it anyway.** It won't kill you. (We promise.) And your quiet, pleasant actions will go a lot further than a grimace or a sarcastic comment like, **"Sheesh, Mom! Even prisoners don't have to be tortured with THIS gunk. Where's the cereal?"**

If you lose your parents' TRUST, it's going to take a while to get it back.

And by *a while*, we don't mean a day or two.

The nature of the "crime" (what you did to betray their trust) will determine how long it will be before your parents can trust you again.

You may not realize this, but **your parents' trust is the most important thing you can have.** If they trust you, your teens will be great. If they don't, get used to staying home on Friday and Saturday nights. It's that simple.

Your parents will lose their trust in you if they . . .

- catch you in a deliberate lie
- find drugs in your room or smell alcohol on your breath
- **expect you to be someplace, then find out you weren't there**
- spend a lot of time with friends of "questionable" morals or character

You can't regain broken trust through logic, pleading, or promises.

T-I-M-E and good behavior are the only ways to get it back.

Parents try to intentionally embarrass their children ...NOT!

Some teens think being seen with their parents is cruel and unusual punishment. They're constantly looking for ways to avoid being caught with them in places where others could connect them. It's true, **parents can do things that will make you feel like telling anyone in earshot you're adopted.** Stuff like:

- Yelling at you in public. (Some do have tempers.)
- Saying "inappropriate" (stupid) things.
- Dressing funny.

When parents have done something that embarrasses you, fight the urge to hide.

And realize . . .

- They probably didn't do it on purpose (though this is not *always* the case).
- They still need time alone with you, so don't shut them out completely.
- Kindness will probably change their behavior faster than acting angry.
- **If people are busy thinking your parents are weird, they aren't thinking you are.**
- Parents like to have fun, too. Let them.

Talk to your parents before something happens. Let them know you want to spend time with them, but are sometimes embarrassed by what they do or say (be specific). Don't feel bad about letting them know your feelings, and remember to tell them that you love them.

Ask your parents to help you establish some important GOALS.

Want to be successful? It all begins with setting goals and creating a strategy to *meet* those goals.

Enlist your mom's and dad's help in determining your strengths. Share your desires with them. If you want to be a lawyer, tell them. If you feel the Lord is calling you to be a teacher, share it. You feel a pull toward the mission field? Explain that to your folks. After all, they can't help you meet your goals if they don't know where your heart is.

After you've discussed a few career ideas, write them down in a special notebook. Then **ask your parents how you can meet those goals.** For example, if you want to be an astronaut, jot down the names of the math and science classes you ought to take before you graduate from high school, then list several colleges or universities that would best prepare you for this career. Next, contact those colleges and ask for a free catalogue. File everything.

And if your desires begin to change? That's okay! (You're *normal!*) Just track them in your special notebook. **You'll reach your goals a lot faster than friends who don't take the time to sit down and sift through their abilities and hopes for the future.**

When I (Susie) was in the fifth grade, I knew I was interested in writing. Our teacher assigned written and oral book reports. I volunteered early so I could get mine over with. Know why? Because after I reported on a library book I had to read, I then got to work on what I really wanted to do: writing my own book!

That year, I wrote a book called *The Magic Eraser.* By the time everyone had completed their oral reports, I was finished with my book, and read it to the class.

Since I began to realize how much I enjoyed writing, I set some goals. In junior high, I enrolled in journalism. I later joined the newspaper staff. For fun, I mailed off some things I'd written to a Christian youth magazine. Imagine my surprise when I received a check in the mail with a letter explaining when my work would be published!

Then I joined the high-school newspaper staff. Later, I became the advertising manager . . . all the while free-lancing for a variety of Christian teen magazines. I took creative writing my senior year of high school, then headed for college.

By this time I knew this desire to write was more than something I enjoyed doing. It was also a *calling* from the Lord. **I knew God wanted me to communicate for Him. . . through speaking and writing.**

So, obeying that call, I majored in communications, grabbed a double minor in English and creative writing, and later received my master's degree in creative writing.

It all started with focusing on my strengths, looking at my desires, and setting some goals. I consistently asked God to guide me, and with my parents' support, I headed confidently toward fulfilling that desire for my life.

Why some parents don't like loud MUSIC.

• It reminds them of when they were able to blare *their* music, and they're jealous they can't do it anymore.

• **The hairs in your dad's ears vibrate and tickle him.**

• They're afraid your pastor will stop in for a visit when you've got it cranked to nineteen!

• **Old age** already makes it difficult for them to remember what they're doing—noisy distractions only make it worse.

• They're tired of spackling and repainting your bedroom ceiling after it cracks.

• **It really does hurt their ears.**

• They think you're using loud music to deliberately annoy them and rebel against their authority. (Are they right?)

When am I old enough to group date, double date, or single date? How do I talk to my parents about this subject? How far is too far to go physically on a date?

Great questions! But obviously they need more space than what this book is designed for! If you want the whole scoop and nothing but the scoop, check out three books we've written on the entire subject of **opposite-sex relationships:**

1. *Getting Ready for the Guy/Girl Thing* is for guys and girls eleven to fourteen (or so). Good stuff to keep you from **embarrassing yourself** when you're with the opposite sex.

2. *What Hollywood Won't Tell You About SEX, LOVE, and DATING* is for teens older than fourteen. When you're ready to start spending more time with the opposite sex—or if your mind is almost **always thinking about them**—this is a must read.

3. *258 Great Dates While You Wait* is for any teen who needs some absolutely, incredibly **phenomenal ideas** on how to spend good, quality time with the opposite sex. (Actually, there are way more than 258 ideas!)

CONFIDE in your parents.

An amazing thing happens when you hit your teen years. All of a sudden you feel as though you can't tell your parents anything. You fear getting a lecture, or worse, some sort of punishment.

Sadly, some parents *will* use any new information to keep their kids under a tighter grip. Most parents, however, want their relationship with their child to grow. No, they know they can't hope to be best buds; occasionally they may have to wear the black hat. But they *do* want to be involved in discussions when there are bigger decisions to be made. Just like a friend would.

When you ask a parent for advice, something special happens. Their entire existence is validated. What they hoped would happen has happened. Their years of experience are being relied on by someone they love more than life itself.

Along with the day-to-day stuff, **there are two things you REALLY should discuss with your folks: decisions and secrets.**

Decisions are easy. You ask their opinion, weigh their wisdom against your own, then act. Sometimes it's easy, like buying a car. Other times your future is at stake. Perhaps it's a college choice . . . or maybe the biggest choice of all—whom to marry.

Secrets, on the other hand, are tough to confide. But **the more secrets you have from your parents, the more distant your relationship will be.**

If you've been burned in the past, or you're not sure how your parents will respond if you tell them a secret, we want to challenge you to give them another chance. No, not another chance to burn you, but an honest chance to see your heart. Over breakfast or at bedtime, try a conversation like this:

"Dad, Mom, the older I get, the more I experience. Some good, some not so good. In the past when I've told you stuff, I've either received a lecture or got in trouble.

"I really want to have a close relationship with you, but it's tough for me to talk when your response isn't what I think it should be.

"I'm a good kid. Can you please think through your response when I talk to you about something sensitive?"

Though this may seem corny or unrealistic in your present circumstance, please hear this: Your friendships will change about every two or three years. In fact, it's likely you'll only have a few "lifetime friends." Your parents, however, will be around for many, many years. **Believe it or not, chances are you'll actually want to be close to your parents as you grow older.** Our advice is to build up the habit of confiding in your folks in as many areas as you can. You won't regret it.

Parents will sometimes be UNFAIR.

No one wants to be treated unfairly—especially if it means he doesn't get to do what he wants to do.

But this much is certain: **Mom and Dad will be unfair at several times in your life. They'll . . .**

- Pay more attention to other siblings.
- **Change their minds for no reason.**
- Occasionally not keep their word.
- Unknowingly compare you with others to try to motivate you to do better.
- **Invade your privacy.**
- Expect you to respond immediately when they want you to do something (instead of waiting for the commercial).

And this is the short list!

So what's our advice?

Don't be surprised when it happens. Remember, you've been warned.

Try not to put your parents in the POORHOUSE.

Making unreasonable demands on your folks is not only unkind, **but it makes them feel pretty lousy.**

Will your life fall apart if you don't get those name-brand tennis shoes, or that starter jacket you've demanded? Nah. Parents love to give their kids stuff . . . **but keep it in perspective.**

Should your parents have anything to say about what FRIENDS you spend time with?

You've heard the phrase, *You can pick your friends, you can pick your nose . . . but you can't pick your friend's nose*, right? (Well, maybe not. It has nothing to do with this topic, but we've always wanted to use it in one of our books. This seemed as good as place as any.)

By now you are probably well beyond the days when your parents picked your friends. But it probably hasn't prevented them from commenting on your choice of friends through the years.

(If you've never had a problem in this area, you can skip to the next section.)

Why should parents care about who you hang out with? After all, *they're* not the ones spending time with them—*you* are!

Though parents shouldn't try to control every aspect of their child's life, some do. That's a shame. Teens need to be allowed to experience a measure of freedom in many areas—within limits. Who you hang around with is usually one of them. But does that mean they shouldn't ever say anything about your friends? Does it mean they don't trust you when they do?

My (Greg) best grade-school friend started getting into the wrong crowd in seventh grade. He wanted to be part of the cool group. He grew his hair the way the group did, dressed the same, talked the same—and went to the same parties. In a short period of time, he was a totally changed person.

I went my way, he went his. Though I certainly made tons of mistakes during my teenage years, this guy did too. Only his mistakes cost him—

BIG TIME. His crowd popped pills that did weird things to your brain. They drank, smoked, and all the rest. After graduation, I became a Christian (thankfully!); he kept up his old habits. One year later I received a phone call. My boyhood friend, the guy I shared hundreds of great times with . . . was dead. Drugs and alcohol had formed a deadly mixture. Some thought it could have been a suicide. I spoke at his funeral. It was one of the saddest days of my life.

Perhaps if his parents would have questioned his friendships at an early age he'd still be alive. We'll never know.

Do you realize your parents have made an investment in you? If yours are Christians, they probably began praying for you before you were born. They changed hundreds of dirty diapers, clipped your toenails, brushed your teeth, washed tons of your dirty laundry, spent thousands on clothes (that you outgrew in three months) and food (that you didn't eat until you became a teenager). They read stories, sang songs, played games, prayed still more, and read books on how to be a better parent. They've made a sizable investment in you through the years, haven't they? (It's okay to agree, no one's looking.)

Then one day, along comes a new friend, someone whose parents have not made such a sizable investment. As a result, your friend's moral foundation isn't as strong as yours. Suddenly, you're spending all of your time with this person. Your behavior is changing. You may begin saying hurtful things to your folks. **They sense you pulling away, changing, become a different person.** And they can trace it back to when you first started hanging around this friend.

Tell us: Don't your parents have some right to question the value of that person's influence when you begin to belittle their love, protection, and authority?

We've known dozens of teens who didn't think so. They denied their parents any right to question the choices they'd made about friends. In a matter of months, the parents' years of investing in that child crumbled before their eyes. One friend, or perhaps a group of friends—and often a friend of the opposite sex—put a wedge between parent and child that took months and years to overcome.

It's risky being a parent. You can't control your children . . . you don't even want to. You know your children need to make their own decisions as they grow older. Sometimes your children will make decisions with painful consequences.

If you'll pardon the digression for a moment, this is exactly the dilemma God is in. He has invested much more in us than our parents, yet He knows that true love allows a maturing person to make up her own mind about whether she wants to remain under His authority. The consequence is that millions walk away from His love and free offer of eternal salvation. God's love lets them go. It hurts Him, but He has no other choice. He cares for His creation too much to control them.

Most parents do, too. But **while you're still under their roof, they cannot help but call your attention to potentially harmful friendships.** Yes, some parents do have a hard time letting go, but most have much purer motives.

The next time your parents question one of your friendships, a group you're hanging around with, an unhealthy relationship you're having with the opposite sex—don't shut them out. Hear them out. You might thank them for it someday.

Your CURFEW depends on you.

Like a lot of other questions your parents have about raising you, there's no clear-cut answer in the Bible for this one: "How late should I let my teenager stay out?"

The final decision is up to your parents. So how do they decide? They can rely on their instincts, older friends who have raised teenagers, their own experience as teenagers . . . or **they can look to you.**

So how should you answer?

We hear a few of you thinking, *Three a.m. on Fridays, but ONLY one a.m. on Saturdays—because of church. I gotta be awake to hear the pastor's sermon.*

Nice try.

Like most decisions your parents make, **their feelings** on this subject **won't depend on your opinion, but your actions.**

Are you the type who likes to push rules to the limit? Expect an early curfew.

Do you argue about when you'll do your homework, clean your room, or do your chores? Then forget about negotiating on late-night fun.

Extended curfews are a privilege, not a right. You can't find a midnight curfew anywhere in the "teen bylaws." (Nor can you find any teen bylaws!)

If you want to push and argue everything your parents say, that's between you and them. But if you want the privileges that growing older can bring, being reasonable and responsible will get you a lot further. Guaranteed!

Try to make a wonderful MEMORY for your mom on Mother's Day (and for your dad on Father's Day).

You don't have to be loaded with money to make Mom and Dad happy. Don't think you have to buy her her favorite perfume or take him out to an expensive restaurant to create a special memory. (Though, if you can afford it, those things are nice!)

Contemporary Christian artist Margaret Becker and her older sister decided to do something special for their mom when Maggie was in junior high.

Since the two girls didn't have much money, they got together and made their mom a coupon book. Each coupon could be redeemed for a specific helpful task. For instance, one was for washing the dishes, another for taking out the trash, dusting the furniture, doing the laundry, etc.

According to Maggie, those coupons were the best gift her mom ever received. Why? Because they came from the hearts of two girls who loved their mom. (You can do this same thing for Dad.)

Start thinking now about what you can do to create a terrific memory for your mom and dad next time their special days come around. Why not make a list of ideas? Here are a few to get you started:

- Make a coupon book like Maggie and her sister.
- **Take photos of your dad, mom, and family throughout the year.** About a month before Mother's Day, assemble them in an empty book. Write special things about each picture and why your mom is so important to you (lay it out like a yearbook). Then present it to her on her day.

• Make her breakfast and serve it to her in bed.

• Using a video camera (if you don't have one, you could probably borrow one from someone in your church—or you could even rent one for a weekend) and **film different aspects of your mom's life.** Have each of your family members explain on camera why your mom is important to them. If you have the time, try to interview some of her close friends as well. And if you *really* get into this, set the film to her favorite songs. At the very end of the tape, explain (while looking into the camera) why you love her so much.

Imagine her surprise when you play the video for her on her day. It'll be something she'll treasure forever; she'll probably watch it *at least* a bazillion times!

Time to list a few of your OWN ideas.

____

____

____

____

Don't spread your family SECRETS.

For instance, if your dad snores, chances are he probably doesn't want your circle of friends gabbing about it.

Here are a few other things you might want to keep to yourself:

- your older brother's ingrown toenail
- **Mom hitting menopause**
- your sister's temper tantrums
- **your flossing techniques**
- the fact that you have termites in your home
- the stain on the carpet from the time your little brother threw up
- **your Uncle Ben's prison record**
- anything related to bankruptcy

When your parents have asked you several times to do something, be CAREFUL how you respond.

Here are some lines that NEVER work:

- "Yeah, yeah, yeah. I already heard ya!"
- "You think I'm deaf?"
- "Well, Dad, I'd *like* to clean out the garage, I really would, but the truth is I have a lot more important things to do than rearranging the family's junk."
- **"My room isn't really messy, it's just organizationally impaired."**
- "So what if the grass in our front lawn is knee-high? It'll greatly aid my little brother's imagination when he's playing jungle hunt."

And here are a few lines that might work:

- "Mom, I know I'm supposed to have my room clean by tonight, but I really want to go to the football game. Can we compromise? How 'bout if I clean it tomorrow morning before soccer practice—and just to show you how grateful I am—I'll take out all the trash, too."
- "Dad, I had to finish up our history project at the library today. It's a group thing, and the other kids were counting on me. **Since I didn't get a chance to mow the lawn today, I promise I'll do it right after school tomorrow.** Is this okay?"
- "I realize you've asked me several times to do that, but the truth is, I *hate* this chore. Can you help me think of some ideas to make it more bearable?"

Be willing to go the extra MILE when one of your parents is sick.

Because Mom and Dad aren't superheroes, they get sick. One of them may even experience a serious illness that will affect your entire family. That's when you have a few choices to make.

YOU MAY FEEL LIKE:

Throwing in the towel. After all, you're not a miracle worker. What could *you* possibly do to make a difference, anyway? Maybe your dad is going to be confined to a wheelchair. Obviously, that means no more tackle football in the backyard. And you won't be jogging together anymore. So why not just give up? Throw in the towel, and drop off of the track team.

WHAT WILL HELP MOST:

Keeping a positive attitude. No, you don't have a degree in medicine or psychology, but deciding to maintain a cheerful attitude will shout **VOLUMES** to your dad. After all, it's harder on *him* than it is on *you.* He's the one who's suffering, remember? So smile. And keep smiling. And continue toward your goals. Make your sick parent proud—in spite of his illness.

YOU MAY FEEL LIKE:

Turning your back on God. After all, you're a good kid. How could He let this happen to your family? You have friends who are always in trouble, yet they never seem to hurt or suffer. So, you stop giving your tithes and offerings at church. And you slack off on your attendance. You'll show God!

WHAT WILL HELP MOST:

Deepening your relationship with God and with church friends.

You need the Lord's strength **NOW** more than ever. So why walk away from Him? No, you don't understand what's going on, but guess what? It's not your responsibility to understand. Relying on God's strength, *accept without understanding!* (REPEAT: Rely on God's strength—not your own.)

God never promised us an easy life, did He? He **DID** promise to stick close and pour himself (and that includes His peace, His strength, His comfort, His wisdom) into our lives.

And those church friends? Even though they don't understand, you need their fellowship. Sometimes just being around other Christians your age is a comfort.

Oh, yeah . . . one more thing: Memorize 2 Corinthians 4:8–9. (We'll even include it so you won't have to look it up.)

"We are pressed on every side by troubles, but not crushed and broken. We are perplexed because we don't know why things happen as they do, but we don't give up and quit. We are hunted down, but God never abandons us. We get knocked down, but we get up again and keep going." (TLB)

YOU MAY FEEL LIKE:

Throwing a pity party. Guess who the first guests will be? Anger, bitterness, and withdrawal. After all, no one else understands. Life's not fair!

WHAT WILL HELP MOST:

Throwing yourself into the lives of others. And your first target should be your parents. Throw yourself into helping them. "Mom, is there anything I can pick up at the store for you?"

"Dad, do you need gas in the car?"

"I just emptied the trash. Anything else you need done?"

"Got any ironing I can tackle?"

By concentrating on the needs of *others*, you'll forget about yourself. And isn't that **the equation for genuine joy:**

Jesus first.
Others second.
Yourself last.

Don't play on the ROOF.

When you were little, your dad would never let you walk around on the roof (or take other dangerous chances) unless you were right next to him, holding his hand. His fear, of course, was that you'd break your neck if he weren't there to protect you. Then you'd either die or be in a wheelchair for the rest of your life—and your dad would have to take care of you for the rest of **HIS** life. (Basically, it would have been a bad deal either way.)

His concerns haven't faded now that you're older. Whenever you're in any potentially dangerous position (unless it's right next to him on the roof while helping him put up Christmas lights), he sees visions of you lying sprawled out on the ground—not moving, but calling his name.

Nothing is worth putting your dad through his worst nightmare. Stay off the roof.

75 If you don't have a dad, PRAY for a healthy male role model.

Perhaps your dad died, or left your family. Though he can't be replaced, **God can bring other godly men into your life.**

Is there an uncle whom you admire? Or a close family friend? What about a solid Christian from your church? Ask the Lord to bring someone like that to mind. Then (with your mom's permission), **approach him and ask if he'd pray for you.**

Later, ask if you can seek his advice on things where you need a male perspective. With God's blessing, this man can become a **positive influence** on your life.

Start family TRADITIONS.

Most families have a few traditions. Many times they revolve around the holidays (though they don't have to). For instance, my family (Susie) always has a big formal dinner on Christmas Eve (and we always have ham), then we exchange gifts. Afterward, we all drive around looking at Christmas lights.

Does your family have any special traditions? Do you plan something special for Thanksgiving? Or maybe a Fourth of July picnic?

If you don't have traditions, suggest to your parents that you work together to create some. Start with holidays, because they're the easiest to remember.

Keep in mind: the best traditions are memorable. If they're something everyone enjoys doing, they will always be remembered. And traditions don't have to be expensive. Sometimes the most special traditions are actually pretty ordinary. For instance, when I was a little girl, my family always got ice cream after church on Wednesday nights. It never cost much, and it was something we all looked forward to.

Ask your parents if *their* families had any traditions that were especially meaningful when they were growing up. You might want to use some of those ideas to get started.

What do your parents WANT for you?

Here's what it all comes down to: Your parents do what they do because they want something for you. But just what is that something?

They want your life to be better than theirs.

They definitely don't want it to be worse, and more than likely they don't want it to be the same, either. They've probably made a few mistakes, learned from them, and don't want you to feel the pain—or embarrassment—they felt trying to dig their way out.

Do you know how an airplane or the Space Shuttle gets to its destination? It makes mistakes! That's right. Whether the plane is being manually steered or on automatic pilot, it can't help but go off course. But when it begins to veer slightly to the left or right, the pilot (or automatic pilot), sets it back on course. Nearly one hundred percent of the time it arrives at its destination. And that's exactly what your parents want for you.

So what is that hoped-for destination?

- Eternity in heaven.
- **A strong, personal faith in Jesus.**
- A heart to help those less fortunate.
- **The desire to use your gifts and talents to the best of your ability.**
- A life that is (mostly) unstained by the consequences of sin.
- Contentment, not just happiness.

- **True riches, not just wealth.**

All of that is a pretty tall order, isn't it?

Tall, but not impossible. You see, your parents think that if they can just motivate you at the right time and in the right way, you'll have the desire and inner strength it takes to pursue the abundant life Jesus talked about in John 10:10.

Is there anything wrong with wanting your child to move in this direction? Of course not! **You'll want the same for your kids.**

That's why you need to look at your parents' motives for what they do. All they really want is for you to reach these goals.

Here's the question of the hour: Do you want to help them help you? It's up to you.